MAMMALS
of
California and Nevada

Selected examples and related species

E. Lendell Cockrum
and
Yar Petryszyn

Drawings by
Sandy Truett and Helen A. Wilson

Published by
Treasure Chest Publications, Inc.
P.O. Box 5250
Tucson AZ 85703-0250

Design and Typesetting by
Casa Cold Type, Inc.

Cover Design by
Kathleen A. Koopman

Cover Illustration by
Deboragh McDonnell

Printed in the U.S.A.

Printing 10 9 8 7 6 5 4 3 2 1

ISBN 0-918080-72-X

Information symbols

One or more of the following symbols is given with each of the major species listed in this manual.

Time of Activity

 Diurnal: active during the daytime.

 Nocturnal: active at night.

 Crepuscular: generally active at dawn or at dusk.

Status of Populations

 Eliminated in this area.

 Rare or endangered in part or all of this area.

 A game animal or fur-bearer subject to regulations as to seasons and limits.

For current information concerning rare and endangered species and laws and seasons for hunting and trapping, contact your local federal or state officials as listed in your telephone directory or contact:

United States Fish and Wildlife Service, Western Region
Eastside Federal Complex
911 N S 11th Avenue
Portland, OR 97232-4181

California Department of Fish and Game
Room 1225, 1414 Ninth Street
Sacramento, CA 95814

Nevada Department of Wildlife
Box 10678
Reno, NV 89520

Contents

A Word from the Authors

This guide is designed to help interested novices add to their knowledge of native mammals. It was not designed as a technical or semitechnical reference. Persons desiring more information should consult one or more of the books listed in the Suggested Readings at the end of this guide.

This book will be most useful in California and Nevada.

At least 175 different species of native terrestrial mammals have occurred in these states within historic times. However, only about 79 are usually recognized as being obviously distinct. These we have listed as "major types." For example, most novices have little difficulty distinguishing between a Round-tailed ground squirrel and a Golden-mantled ground squirrel or between a California leaf-nosed bat and a Brazilian free-tailed bat, even though they have never seen or heard of these mammals. Such species are obviously different.

In contrast, even professional mammalogists often have difficulty quickly distinguishing among a Cliff chipmunk, California chipmunk, Long-eared chipmunk, and others. Because all chipmunks are very similar in size, shape, and color, only close attention to minor differences reveals that they are different species.

In this book, each major type is illustrated, and, for each, the common and scientific names, some major identifying features, measurements, habitats, and highlights of life habits are given. The common names and scientific names used here are our interpretations of current literature. Most conform with the 1987 *Checklist of Vertebrates of the United States, the U.S. Territories, and Canada*, a publication of the United States Fish and Wildlife Service (see Banks et al., 1987, in the Suggested Readings). Related species are only briefly mentioned at the end of the book.

The mammals are grouped into major biological categories (bats, rodents, hoofed mammals, etc.) and are listed in the sequence normally assumed by biologists as indicating relationships.

Measurements are given in both English and metric units. Values are representative, not definitive. As in all animals, including man, individual variations make a single value almost meaningless. For instance, the small size of a young animal, the large size of an old, obese individual, or the sexual dimorphism that occurs in such species as the Wapiti (adult males are much larger than adult females) all contribute to variability. However, if the values given here are interpreted as being plus or minus 10%, then most variation of adults will be included. Measurements have been compiled from a number of sources including specimens in the Mammal Collection at the University of Arizona. Especially useful were the books by Hall listed in the Suggested Readings.

A distribution map shows the general region in which a mammal occurs or has occurred in the past. Notes on habitat indicate special situations within this range where the species is usually found.

Some native mammals have not done well in their interaction with human use of the land. A few have been exterminated, at least locally. Others have prospered, becoming even more numerous with human modifications of the area.

Several nonnative mammals, both domestic and wild, have been introduced. Some are now the dominant mammals of various microhabitats. A partial list of domestic mammals that have been introduced includes cows, horses, burros, goats, sheep, house cats, and dogs. Some have become so well established that they are now essentially "native." The Virginia opossum, the Black rat, the Norway rat, and the House mouse are examples. Others have become established only locally. These include the Fox squirrel and the Eastern gray squirrels that live in various city parks, the burros that thrive on various rangelands, the Eastern cottontail, the European rabbit, and the Nutria.

Many other exotic species have been released, either accidentally or purposefully. A few of these are surviving locally, often in a semidomestic state. The well-advertised wild animal "farms" are obvious examples.

Much of this material was originally published by Cockrum as part of the *Mammals of the Southwest*. Several people aided in the preparation of this manuscript. Special thanks are due Joe C. Truett for his permission to use Sandy's drawings and to Helen A. Wilson for producing additional drawings. We also thank Anne Gondor for converting sketch maps of species distribution into publishable maps.

E. Lendell Cockrum and
Yar Petryszyn
1993

The Mammals

Virginia opossum

Didelphis virginiana

Order Marsupialia   **Family Didelphidae**

Identifying Features

The Virginia opossum is about the size of a house cat. Its long, hairless tail is prehensile (like that of many monkeys), the snout is long, and the ears are naked and black. The face is white; the body is covered with long, shaggy, coarse, gray hair.

Measurements

Total length, 30 inches (760 mm); tail, 12 inches (300 mm); hind foot, 2 inches (50 mm); ear, 1 inch (25 mm); weight, 10 pounds (4.5 kg).

Habitat

Opossums were introduced into southern California about 1900. They are now widely established, especially in agricultural areas, lowlands, and along streams.

Life Habits

Generally feeding at night, the opossum is active throughout the year. Females give birth to poorly developed young that make their way to the marsupial pouch where further development occurs. They eat almost anything available: roots, stems, fruits, melons, carrion, insects, eggs, frogs, birds, and other foods. Opossums are slow and deliberate in their movements, thus they are often run over on highways.

Virginia opossum

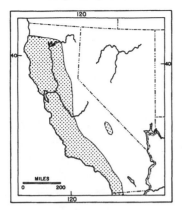

Vagrant shrew

Sorex vagrans

Order Insectivora   **Family Soricidae**

Identifying Features

This tiny mammal has a long snout and short, dense, velvetlike blackish to brownish fur. The belly is tinged with brown or red. The tail is the same color above and below. The eyes and ears are so reduced that they are difficult to see. The numerous teeth have reddish enamel.

Measurements

Total length, 4 inches (100 mm); tail, 1.6 inches (40 mm); hind foot, 0.5 inch (12 mm); weight, 0.3 ounce (8 g).

Habitat

These shrews live in pine forests where they are common along moist streamsides, especially in dense humus and plant cover.

Life Habits

Shrews are active at night and during the day. They usually eat about 75% of their body weight in food each day. Insects make up most of their diet, but earthworms and even small mice are eaten. Shrews spend their lives in a small area, probably smaller than a small city lot (4000 square feet, 370 square meters). One litter is born each summer after a gestation period of about 20 days. Two to nine (usually four to six) young are born in a litter. *See related species 1-10.*

Vagrant shrew

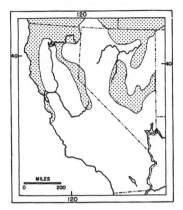

Broad-footed mole

Scapanus latimanus

Order Insectivora   **Family Talpidae**

Identifying Features

The mole is greatly modified for underground life. The body is stout and has no evident neck. The snout is elongated, external ears are absent, the eyes are extremely reduced. The forelimbs are short; the hands are broad and shovellike and have strong nails. The fur is short, dense, and velvetlike. The short tail is almost hairless.

Measurements

Total length, 6.9 inches (175 mm); tail, 1.4 inches (35 mm); hind foot, 0.9 inch (22 mm); weight, 3.2 ounces (85 g).

Habitat

These moles are found in areas of deep, damp soils, often in meadows and lawns. They occur from sea level to about 8000 feet (2440 m).

Life Habits

Broad-footed moles are active throughout the year and may feed at any time of the day. They feed on grubs, earthworms, and other invertebrates that are captured in the extensive underground feeding tunnel systems. Moles are most evident in lawns and gardens where mounds of excavation debris and ridges of raised vegetation or earth are highly visible. *See related species 11-13.*

Broad-footed mole

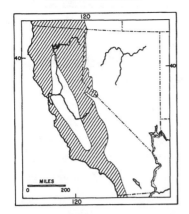

California leaf-nosed bat

Macrotus californicus

Order Chiroptera   **Family Phyllostomidae**

Identifying Features

This bat has a well-developed wedge-shaped nose leaf (flap of flesh growing up from the tip of the nose), large ears that extend forward of the tip of the nose, and are joined at their bases. The long interfemoral membrane (skin between the legs) is naked and encloses the tail.

Measurements

Total length, 3.8 inches (95 mm); tail, 1.3 inches (32 mm); hind foot, 0.6 inch (15 mm); ear, 1.3 inches (32 mm); forearm, 2 inches (50 mm); weight, 0.4 ounce (12 g).

Habitat

These bats occur in the desert below 4000 feet (1220 m).

Life Habits

These bats are active throughout the year. They are colonial, with groups of up to several hundred spending the day in warm caves or mine tunnels. On warm nights, they leave to feed on night-flying insects. On cold nights, they remain in their roost. This is a tropical species that never evolved the ability to hibernate. Mating occurs in the fall and, after a long, slow period of development, a single young is born the following June. The young grows rapidly, reaching adult size in about six weeks.

California leaf-nosed bat

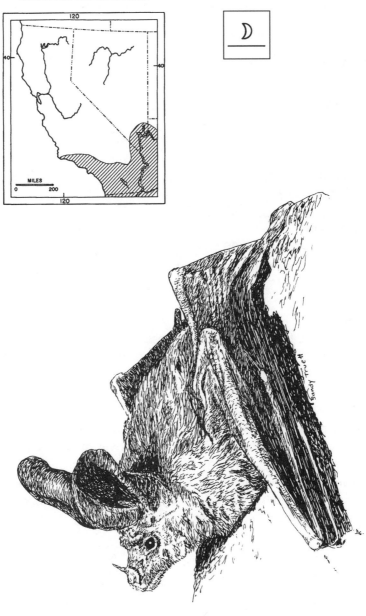

Long-tongued bat

Choeronycteris mexicana

Order Chiroptera   **Family Phyllostomidae**

Identifying Features

Long-tongued bats have a nose leaf. The head is modified for a diet of nectar: the rostrum (snout) is elongated, the ears are reduced, and the tongue is long and extensible. The extremely short tail extends only about half the length of the short inter-femoral membrane.

Measurements

Total length, 3.5 inches (90 mm); tail, 1.6 inches (40 mm); hind foot, 0.5 inch (12 mm); ear, 0.7 inch (17 mm); weight, 0.6 ounce (18 g).

Habitat

During the day, Long-tongued bats roost, often singly, but sometimes in small groups, in the twilight zone of caves or mine tunnels.

Life Habits

In their normal range (Baja California, southern Arizona, mainland Mexico), these bats feed on the nectar of various agaves and cacti. During the late spring and early summer, females move northward (to the mountains of southern Arizona) or to higher elevations in Mexico. A single young is usual. In California, they are only rare visitors, perhaps being driven north by drought or storms.

Long-tongued bat

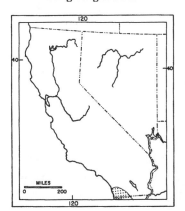

Little brown bat

Myotis lucifugus

Order Chiroptera   **Family Vespertilionidae**

Identifying Features

This plain-nosed bat has no outgrowths on its nose or lips. Its long
tail is entirely surrounded by the interfemoral membrane. The ears
are short, never extending more than 0.3 inch (7 mm) beyond the
nose when folded forward. The tragus (fleshy outgrowth at the
base of the ear opening) ends in a sharp rather than a blunt point.

Measurements

Total length, 3.3 inches (84 mm); tail, 1.5 inches (38 mm); hind
foot, 0.4 inch (10 mm); ear, 0.6 inch (15 mm); forearm, 1.5 inches
(38 mm); weight, 0.3 ounce (9 g). Weights vary to 40%, depending
on time of year (heaviest in fall before hibernation or in early
summer in gravid females).

Habitat

Little brown bats are generally associated with forests.

Life Habits

During the summer, Little brown bats feed on night-flying insects,
storing fat that enables them to hibernate during the cold months.
Winter roosts (hibernal) are in cold (not freezing) caves or tunnels. During spring months, females move to maternity colonies
where a single young is born. Banding studies reveal that some
bats live as long as 23 years. *See related species 14-20.*

Little brown bat

Silver-haired bat

Lasionycteris noctivagans

Order Chiroptera   **Family Vespertilionidae**

Identifying Features

This plain-nosed bat has a long tail enclosed in an interfemoral membrane, the basal half of which is covered with fur. Among bats, the color is unique—being black—with the tips of many hairs being white. The result is a silvery appearance.

Measurements

Total length, 4 inches (100 mm); tail, 1.7 inches (43 mm); hind foot, 0.4 inch (10 mm); ear, 0.6 inch (15 mm); forearm, 1.6 inches (40 mm); weight, 0.3 ounce (9 g).

Habitat

Silver-haired bats are most common in montane forests at elevations above 4000 feet (1220 m).

Life Habits

These bats feed on small night-flying insects, mainly moths. Feeding generally begins after dark. Usually day roosts are single bats in trees, often under bits of bark or in slight holes. One or two young are born in late June or early July. During cold months, some of these bats migrate down mountains where, on warm nights, they feed; but on cold nights, they remain inactive and hibernate. Others make a north-south seasonal migration, spending summer as far north as southern Canada and winter in the southern United States.

Silver-haired bat

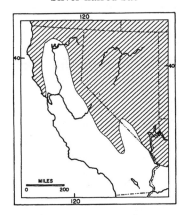

Western pipistrelle

Pipistrellus hesperus

Order Chiroptera   **Family Vespertilionidae**

Identifying Features

This is the smallest bat in the United States. The tail and inter-femoral membrane are relatively long. Each ear has a short, rounded tragus (fleshy vertical growth on lower edge of ear). The color is light, usually a buff gray, with a black mask across the eyes.

Measurements

Total length, 2.8 inches (72 mm); tail, 1.3 inches (32 mm); hind foot, 0.2 inch (5 mm); ear, 0.5 inch (12 mm); forearm, 1.2 inches (30 mm); weight, 0.1 ounce (3 g).

Habitat

This species occurs most commonly in cliff areas. Rock-walled canyons, usually at elevations below 5000 feet (1524 m), are favored homes.

Life Habits

Pipistrelles are generally solitary, roosting in rock crevices in canyon walls. Small groups have been found roosting in crevices in brick buildings and behind window shutters. The evening flight is early, often before sundown. At dusk, these bats feed on small insects captured in flight. Two young per litter are usual and are born in late June or early July. Males generally spend the winter months at lower elevations and actively feed during warm evenings, while females generally move to higher, colder elevations and hibernate.

Western pipistrelle

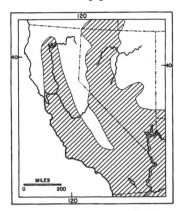

Big brown bat

Eptesicus fuscus

Order Chiroptera   **Family Vespertilionidae**

Identifying Features
This plain-nosed bat has a long tail in a naked interfemoral membrane and short ears. It is sometimes confused with the Little brown bat, from which it differs in being larger and having a blunt tragus. The wing and interfemoral membranes are almost black.

Measurements
Total length, 4 inches (100 mm); tail, 1.5 inches (38 mm); hind foot, 0.4 inch (10 mm); ear, 0.6 inch (15 mm); forearm, 1.9 inches (47 mm); weight, 0.6 ounce (18 g).

Habitat
Big brown bats occur at a wide range of elevations, from sea level to timberline. They live in forests as well as in more open areas.

Life Habits
In the summer, Big brown bats may have day roosts in buildings, hollow trees, and other similar situations. Winters are spent in hibernation in cold rock crevices and caves at higher elevations. Food consists of night-flying insects. Females give birth to one or two young, usually in mid-June. During the fall, bats that spent the summer at low elevations migrate to cooler, higher elevations and hibernate.

Big brown bat

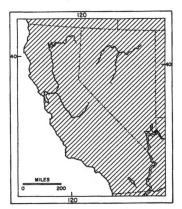

Sandy Truett

Red bat

Lasiurus blossevillii

Order Chiroptera   **Family Vespertilionidae**

Identifying Features
This plain-nosed bat has a long tail enclosed in a fur-covered interfemoral membrane. Its ears are small. The pelage color is bright orange-red to buff, with scattered white-tipped hairs.

Measurements
Total length, 4.3 inches (108 mm); tail, 1.7 inches (43 mm); hind foot, 0.3 inch (7 mm); ear, 0.4 inch (10 mm); forearm, 1.7 inches (43 mm); weight, 0.4 ounce (12 g).

Habitat
Red bats roost in trees, either in forests at high or low elevations or in the scattered trees along streams or washes in the desert or desert grasslands. Those that spend the summer at high elevations migrated down slope or southward to spend the winter.

Life Habits
Red bats feed after dark. They capture flying insects, especially those that occur along the edges of tree stands or over water surrounded by trees. Day roosts are in clumps of leaves in trees. Roosting is solitary except that a female hangs in a cluster with her young. Two to four young are born in late June or early July.

Red bat

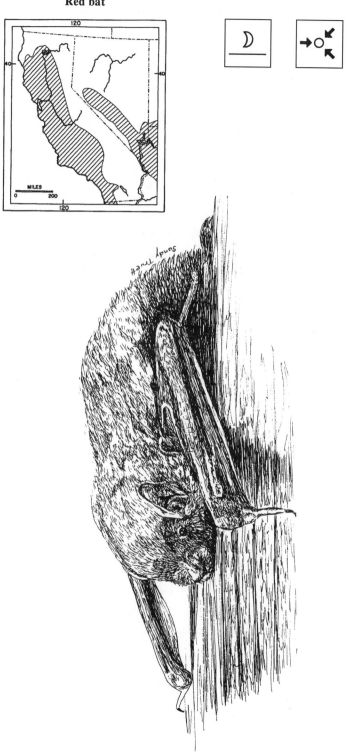

Sandy Truett

Hoary bat

Lasiurus cinereus

Order Chiroptera   **Family Vespertilionidae**

Identifying Features

This bat is similar to the Red bat but is much larger. The back is yellowish to dark brown. It has a frosted (hoary) appearance because many hairs are white-tipped. The interfemoral membrane and the lower surface of the arms and legs are covered with fur.

Measurements

Total length, 5.6 inches (142 mm); tail, 1.9 inches (47 mm); hind foot, 0.5 inch (12 mm); ear, 0.7 inch (17 mm); forearm, 2.1 inches (53 mm); weight, 1 ounce (28 g).

Habitat

Hoary bats are rarely found beyond forests.

Life Habits

Hoary bats feed entirely on night-flying insects. They spend the day roosting singly among the leaves of a tree. Females give birth to two young, generally in late June or early July. Seasonal migrations occur, either from northern areas southward or from high southern mountains down slope to low elevations. Hoary bats are strong fliers and probably can make long flights during a single night.

Hoary bat

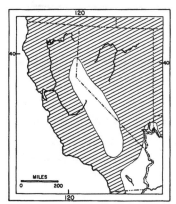

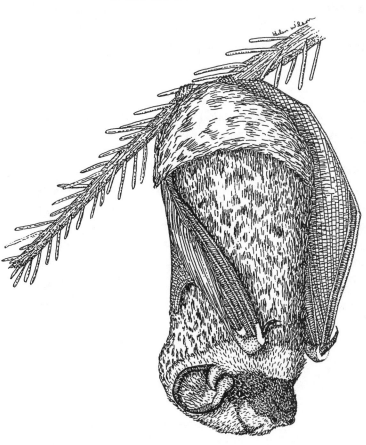

Southern yellow bat

Lasiurus xanthinus

Order Chiroptera   **Family Vespertilionidae**

Identifying Features

This species is similar to the Red bat in size, but differs in color (yellowish to buff with only a few white-tipped hairs), and has only the basal half of the interfemoral membrane covered with hair.

Measurements

Total length, 4.4 inches (110 mm); tail, 2 inches (50 mm); hind foot, 0.4 inch (10 mm); ear, 0.6 inch (15 mm); weight, 0.5 ounce (14 g).

Habitat

Southern yellow bats are associated with palm trees. The range of this species is mostly in Mexico and Central America.

Life Habits

These bats are apparently residents of southern California throughout the year although they are rarely seen in the winter. Day roosts are usually among the dead fronds of palm trees. They feed on night-flying insects after total darkness. Like other tree-roosting species, they hang alone in day roosts. A litter of two young is born in early June.

Southern yellow bat

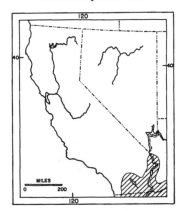 

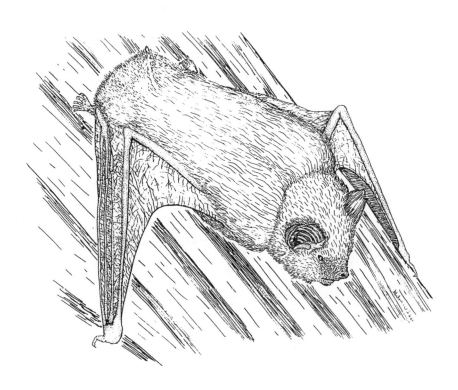

Spotted bat

Euderma maculatum

Order Chiroptera   **Family Vespertilionidae**

Identifying Features

This plain-nosed bat has unique, extremely large, pink-colored ears and black fur that has three dorsal white spots, one on each shoulder and one on the rump. The long tail is enclosed in a naked interfemoral membrane.

Measurements

Total length, 4.3 inches (108 mm); tail, 1.9 inches (47 mm); hind foot, 0.4 inch (10 mm); ear, 1.8 inches (45 mm); forearm, 1.9 inches (47 mm); weight, 0.6 ounce (18 g).

Habitat

Spotted bats are rarely seen and little understood by biologists. They have been taken from hot, low deserts as well as at elevations up to 8000 feet (2440 m). Day roosts are probably in deep rock crevices in high canyon walls.

Life Habits

Spotted bats have been observed only during the warm seasons. Like the related Townsend's big-eared bat, they probably hibernate during the cold seasons and make only a short local trip to the winter roost. Food consists of night-flying insects. This unusual bat is known from a few locations in the western United States and from one location in Chihuahua, Mexico.

Spotted bat

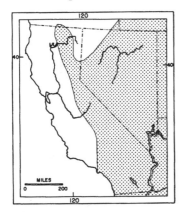

Townsend's big-eared bat

Corynorhinus townsendii

Order Chiroptera   **Family Vespertilionidae**

Identifying Features

This large-eared, plain-nosed bat has a long tail encased in a long, naked interfemoral membrane. It has large ears joined at their inner bases. A pair of prominent glandular lumps occur on each side of the snout.

Measurements

Total length, 4.0 inches (100 mm); tail, 1.8 inches (45 mm); hind foot, 0.4 inch (10 mm); ear, 1.4 inches (35 mm); forearm, 1.6 inches (40 mm); weight, 0.3 ounce (9 g).

Habitat

Townsend's big-eared bats occur in wooded and forested regions. Day roosts are generally in caves, but are sometimes in the attics of buildings.

Life Habits

These bats feed entirely on night-flying insects. They are very agile in flight and can hover and pick insects from plant leaves. During the summer, small numbers (up to 50) congregate in a maternity colony. A single young is born in mid-June. Most winter roosts are in rock crevices at higher elevations. These bats can't tolerate much human disturbance and many populations are now reduced or extinct in areas of high human density. *See related species 21.*

Townsend's big-eared bat

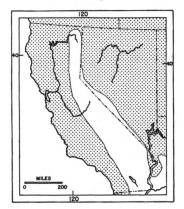

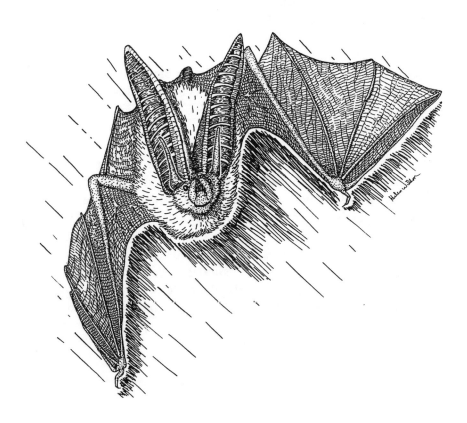

Pallid bat

Antrozous pallidus

Order Chiroptera   **Family Vespertilionidae**

Identifying Features

This plain-nosed, big-eared bat has a long tail encased in a long interfemoral membrane. The body structure is heavy. The color is light, with individual hairs creamy white, tipped with brown or black.

Measurements

Total length, 4.7 inches (120 mm); tail, 1.8 inches (45 mm); hind foot, 0.4 inch (10 mm); ear, 1.2 inches (30 mm); forearm, 2.2 inches (55 mm); weight, 0.7 ounce (20 g).

Habitat

Pallid bats are most common in the lower elevations of southern California but, at least in the summer, occur from high mountains to low deserts.

Life Habits

These bats feed on a variety of large arthropods, including sphinx moths, scarab beetles, grasshoppers, crickets, and scorpions. The prey is carried to a night roost (often a shallow cave, mine tunnel, or house porch) where the soft parts are eaten and the hard wings and legs are dropped. The results are piles of bat droppings and insect parts. During the summer, day roosts are in the attics of buildings, crevices in bridges, or similar places. Winter habits are poorly known, but they probably hibernate in crevices at higher elevations in nearby rocky areas. Two (sometimes one) young are born in June.

Pallid bat

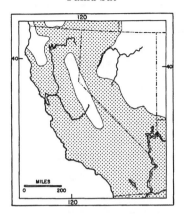

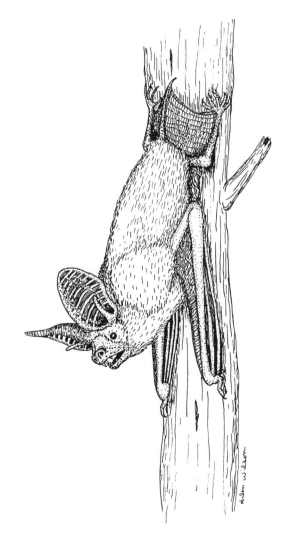

Brazilian free-tailed bat

Tadarida brasiliensis

Order Chiroptera   **Family Vespertilionidae**

Identifying Features
Free-tailed bats have a significant portion of the tail extending posterior to the interfemoral membrane. The flight membranes are dark, thick, and leathery in appearance. The ears are flattened, thickened, and extend forward over the eyes. The hind feet have well-developed tactile hairs.

Measurements
Total length, 4 inches (100 mm); tail, 1.3 inches (32 mm); hind foot, 0.4 inch (10 mm); ear, 0.7 inch (15 mm); forearm, 1.7 inches (43 mm); weight, 0.4 ounce (12 g).

Habitat
Sometimes called Mexican free-tailed bats, these bats are most common at lower elevations in the central valley and southern parts of California but, at least in the summer, occur from high mountains to low deserts.

Life Habits
These colonial bats sometimes congregate in colonies of millions such as the famous group at Carlsbad Caverns, New Mexico. However, most resident summer roosts in this area do not contain more than a few hundred individuals. These feed on night-flying insects, especially small moths. The single young is born in late June. *See related species 22 and 23.*

Brazilian free-tailed bat

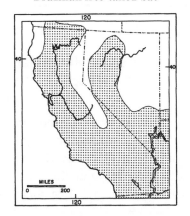

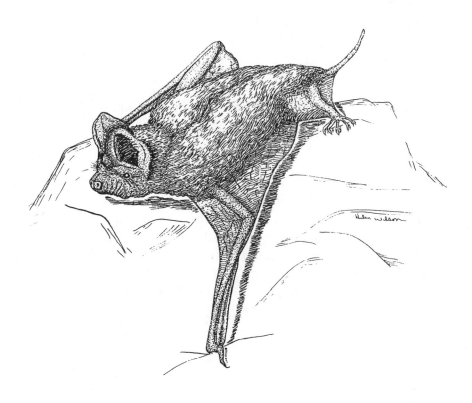

Western mastiff-bat

Eumops perotis

Order Chiroptera   **Family Molossidae**

Identifying Features
Like the Brazilian free-tailed bat, this bat has part of the tail
extending beyond the interfemoral membrane, a thick flight membrane, and tactile hairs on the feet. It differs in being much larger
and in having the low, flattened ears widely fused at the inner
base. This is the largest bat in the area, having a wingspan of about
21 inches (530 mm).

Measurements
Total length, 7.2 inches (185 mm); tail, 2.2 inches (55 mm); hind
foot, 0.7 inch (15 mm); ear, 1.6 inches (40 mm); weight, 2.1
ounces (60 g).

Habitat
Western mastiff-bats are usually found in desert areas with high
rocky cliffs that are near large bodies of permanent water.

Life Habits
These large bats feed entirely on night-flying insects. Day roosts
are small colonies (up to 50 individuals) hanging in rock crevices
high above a canyon floor. A few roosts have been found in the
attics of two-story buildings. These bats have such narrow wings
that they cannot take off in flight from a flat surface but must
climb up some surface, then drop, set their wings, and become
airborne. The single young is born in late June or early July.

Western mastiff-bat

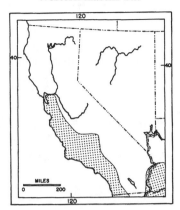 

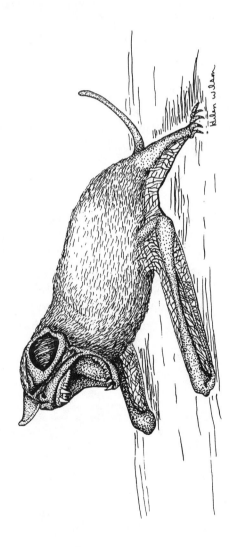

Pika

Ochotona princeps

Order Lagomorpha   **Family Ochotonidae**

Identifying Features

About the size of a guinea pig, this is a small, short-eared, short-legged rabbitlike mammal that has a short tail hidden by the fur. The upper parts are grayish to buff in color. The underparts are lighter and are washed with buff.

Measurements

Total length, 8 inches (200 mm); tail, 0.6 inch (15 mm); hind foot, 1.2 inches (30 mm); ear, 1 inch (25 mm); weight, 4.4 ounces (125 g).

Habitat

North American Pikas live in higher mountains in close association with rock slides. In this region, they are most common in the higher elevations of the Sierra Nevada Mountains.

Life Habits

Pikas are active during the day. They define territories by characteristic calls (whistles) and scent marks. Food consists of various green plants that are eaten or harvested, spread on rocks to dry, and stored for use in the winter season. This stored "hay" is well-hidden in dry places that are readily reached during the winter months when green plants are dead or covered by ice and snow. Two to five (generally three) naked, blind young are born in a fur-lined nest in May or June. They reach adult size by midsummer.

Pika

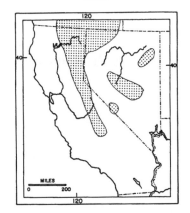

Nuttall's cottontail

Sylvilagus nuttallii

Order Lagomorpha   **Family Leporidae**

Identifying Features
This medium-sized cottontail has relatively short ears, the inner surfaces of which are densely haired. It is usually the only cottontail present in its range. Other species occur in the lower valleys or low desert.

Measurements
Total length, 15.6 inches (400 mm); tail, 1.3 inches (32 mm); hind foot, 4 inches (100 mm); ear, 2.4 inches (62 mm); weight, 2.5 pounds (1.1 kg).

Habitat
These cottontails are common in sagebrush areas, usually at elevations above 4000 feet (1220 m).

Life Habits
Cottontails eat various grasses, herbs, and other green vegetation. They are most active in early morning and late evening, but become almost completely nocturnal during the summer. After a gestation of about four weeks, the young are born in the warmer months. Three or four litters, each consisting of four to seven young, are born in an underground fur-lined nest. The young are hairless, blind, and helpless at birth. Maturity is reached nine to ten months after birth. *See related species 24-26.*

Nuttall's cottontail

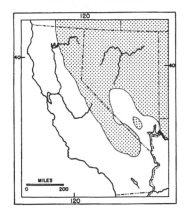

Snowshoe hare

Lepus americanus

Order Lagomorpha   **Family Leporidae**

Identifying Features

This hare has large hind legs and relatively small, black-tipped ears. During summer months, the dorsal color is brownish. In most of its range, the fur is molted and replaced with white hairs during the late fall. The white color is kept during the winter and the ear tips remain black.

Measurements

Total length, 18.7 inches (475 mm); tail, 1.6 inches (40 mm); hind foot, 5.3 inches (135 mm); ear, 3 inches (77 mm); weight, 4 pounds (1.8 kg).

Habitat

Snowshoe hares occur mainly at higher elevations, in bushy areas surrounded by forests. They occur only in northern California and in the Sierra Nevada range.

Life Habits

Snowshoe hares do most of their feeding in the late afternoon or early morning. Several kinds of grasses and herbs make up most of the food. One to seven young (usually four) are born in a litter and more than one litter per year is normal. The young are precocial (born fully haired and with open eyes), and are able to follow their mother within a few minutes after birth.

Snowshoe hare

White-tailed jack rabbit

Lepus townsendii

Order Lagomorpha   **Family Leporidae**

Identifying Features

This hare has both large hind legs and big ears. Its upper parts are grayish, the belly and tail are white. Like the smaller Snowshoe hare, it is white (or nearly white) in the winter and has black tips on the ears throughout the year.

Measurements

Total length, 22.6 inches (575 mm); tail, 3.2 inches (80 mm); hind foot, 5.7 inches (145 mm); ear, 4.3 inches (108 mm); weight, 5.7 pounds (2.5 kg).

Habitat

White-tailed jack rabbits occur in grasslands and sagebrush areas in foothills and lower mountains (from 5000 feet to timberline). They were once common in sagebrush and bunch-grass areas, but are now much reduced in numbers. When the land is heavily used for agriculture or grazing of domestic animals, these rabbits decrease in number and the related Black-tailed jack rabbit becomes more common.

Life Habits

These jack rabbits are similar in habits to the Snowshoe hare. During the summer, they feed on a variety of green plants; during the winter, they feed on buds and bark of shrubs. They are generally active at night, but are seasonally crepuscular (active in late afternoon and early morning). *See related species 27.*

White-tailed jack rabbit

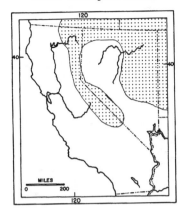

Mountain beaver

Aplodontia rufa

Order Rodentia   **Family Aplodontidae**

Identifying Features

The Mountain beaver has the shape of a giant pocket gopher. Its adaptations for a life underground result in a chunky body, small ears, small eyes, and a short tail. The short legs are stout. The color, which varies from cinnamon to brown, is about the same on the back as on the belly. Old individuals become grayish.

Measurements

Total length, 18 inches (450 mm); tail, 1.5 inches (38 mm); hind foot, 2 inches (50 mm); ear, 1 inch (25 mm); weight, 2.2 pounds (1 kg). Females are about 10% smaller than males.

Habitat

Mountain beavers live in dense thickets and forests, generally restricted to the moist coastal slopes in northwestern California.

Life Habits

Mountain beavers are active throughout the year. Most activity is at night and they rarely leave their burrow system. Burrows are up to 10 inches (250 mm) in diameter and may extend for distances up to 107 yards (100 meters). They feed on a wide variety of plants with the roots, stems, and leaves all eaten. In March or April, a litter of two or three blind young is born in a grass-lined nest. They are not easily kept in captivity.

Mountain beaver

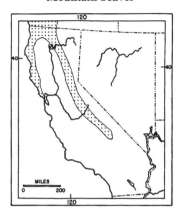

Least chipmunk

Tamias minimus

Order Rodentia   **Family Sciuridae**

Identifying Features
Chipmunks have five evenly spaced longitudinal stripes on the back, three short lateral stripes on each side of the head, and a long, well-haired tail. The belly is usually buff, bright orange, or a grayish yellow. The ears are relatively long and pointed.

Measurements
Total length, 7.7 inches (195 mm); tail, 3.5 inches (90 mm); hind foot, 1.2 inches (30 mm); ear, 0.6 inch (15 mm); weight, 1.8 ounces (50 g).

Habitat
These chipmunks generally live at higher elevations in sagebrush, often some distance from pine trees.

Life Habits
Food consists of many kinds of seeds, berries, fungi, and other plant material. In some areas, juniper berries, acorns, and pine nuts are eaten. Some insects are also eaten. Four to six young per litter is common and some females have two litters in a year. They store various seeds in underground burrows. Most of the cold season is spent in hibernation. *See related species 28-41.*

Least chipmunk

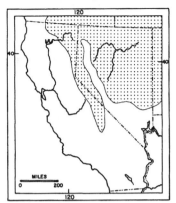

Yellow-bellied marmot

Marmota flaviventris

Order Rodentia   **Family Sciuridae**

Identifying Features

This large, heavyset, ground squirrel-shaped animal has small ears and a short tail. Its color is varied, usually tan or brownish, and often washed with white. An obvious white patch is present between the eyes.

Measurements

Total length, 23.6 inches (600 mm); tail, 8 inches (200 mm); hind foot, 3.2 inches (80 mm); ear, 1 inch (25 mm); weight, to 20 pounds (9 kg). Variations are about 15%, in part because growth continues after adult status is reached.

Habitat

Marmots are usually found in rocky places, often along road cuts in mountainous situations.

Life Habits

Marmots eat plants, especially grasses. They are active during the warm months. In northern mountains, they may be active for only three months of the year. Much fat is stored in the short summer. During the long hibernation, half of the body weight is lost. Adult size is reached in the third year, even though some females have young in their second year. A dominant male defends a territory of about 1.5 acres (0.6 hectares) from other males. Several females and young may live in this territory. A litter of four or five young is common.

Yellow-bellied marmot

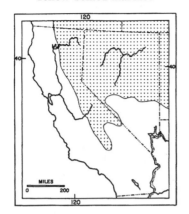

White-tailed antelope squirrel

Ammospermophilus leucurus

Order Rodentia   **Family Sciuridae**

Identifying Features

Antelope squirrels differ from other small squirrellike rodents in that they have a well-developed white stripe extending on each side from the shoulder to the hip and have no central dark stripes. The bushy tail is usually held curved over the back, exposing a white undersurface.

Measurements

Total length, 9.1 inches (230 mm); tail, 3 inches (77 mm); hind foot, 1.5 inches (38 mm); ear, 0.5 inch (12 mm); weight, 4.4 ounces (125 g).

Habitat

Restricted to the low deserts of Nevada and southern California.

Life Habits

These ground squirrels are active most of the year. On cold winter days, they remain underground; on hot summer days, they are most active in the early morning. Food consists of seeds, berries, fruits, insects, and green vegetation. Buds and new growth of mesquite and various cactus fruits are seasonal favorites. They use several short, shallow burrows for protection from heat and enemies as well as for food storage. In February or March, a litter of five to nine young is born in an underground nest chamber. *See related species 42.*

**White-tailed
antelope squirrel**

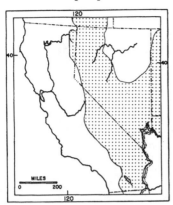

Townsend's ground squirrel

Spermophilus townsendi

Order Rodentia   **Family Sciuridae**

Identifying Features

This is a short-tailed, short-eared ground squirrel that is buff gray in color. The pale spots on the upper surface are usually not evident from a distance. The tail is relatively short, not very bushy, and a dark cinnamon color ventrally.

Measurements

Total length, 9 inches (228 mm); tail, 2 inches (50 mm); hind foot, 1.3 inches (32 mm); ear, 0.3 inch (7 mm); weight, 0.7 pound (300 g).

Habitat

Colonies occur in grassy clearings, especially at the lower edge of the yellow (Ponderosa) pine zone. They are locally common along highways.

Life Habits

These animals end hibernation in early spring, about as soon as snow melts enough to expose green plants. A litter of five to ten young is born soon thereafter. The young grow rapidly, reaching adult size and weight in four months. Adult males become fat about 120 days after emerging from hibernation. They then aestivate (sleep) much of the hot, dry summer. Females and young take longer to become fat, a requirement for successful hibernation. These squirrels are rarely seen aboveground from midsummer until the following spring. *See related species 43 and 44.*

Townsend's ground squirrel

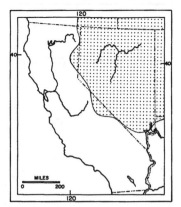

California ground squirrel

Spermophilus beecheyi

Order Rodentia   **Family Sciuridae**

Identifying Features
This large ground squirrel has a long bushy tail. Its upper parts are brown, with buff or white flecks. The sides, from the neck and shoulders to the lower back, are whitish. Colors are darker in the more humid parts of its range.

Measurements
Total length, 18 inches (450 mm); tail, 7 inches (180 mm); hind foot, 2.3 inches (58 mm); ear, 1 inch (25 mm); weight, 1.7 pounds (760 g).

Habitat
These ground squirrels occur in meadows, clearings, and bushy areas from sea level to 8000 feet (2440 m).

Life Habits
These semicolonial animals are inactive between November and February, even in warm places. Activity in the summer is from dawn to dusk. They eat flowers, fruits, seeds, and green growth. Locally, they are agricultural pests, feeding on various crops, even nuts and fruits. A litter of five to eight young is common. Young are born during the summer, with young of the year first appearing aboveground as early as late June and as late as mid-September. *See related species 45.*

California ground squirrel

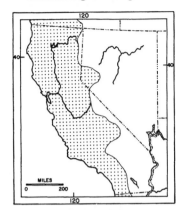

Round-tailed ground squirrel

Spermophilus tereticaudus

Order Rodentia   **Family Sciuridae**

Identifying Features

This small ground squirrel is light colored above, generally some shade of cinnamon. The belly is a lighter shade. The tail is not bushy but is covered with short hairs.

Measurements

Total length, 9.5 inches (240 mm); tail, 2.8 inches (72 mm); hind foot, 1.4 inches (35 mm); ear, 0.2 inch (5 mm); weight, 5 ounces (140 g).

Habitat

Round-tailed ground squirrels live in sandy soils of the lower parts of the Mohave and Colorado deserts.

Life Habits

These squirrels spend the coldest parts of the winter in hibernation. However, during warm periods in midwinter, they may be active aboveground. They are active during the day. In hot weather, most feeding is done in the early morning. During mid-day, they go into their cool underground burrow to escape the heat. They feed on almost any green vegetation, but will eat seeds, flowers, and cactus fruit. One large litter of four to 12 (usually five or six) born in April is usual, but some females may have a second litter in July. *See related species 46.*

Round-tailed
ground squirrel

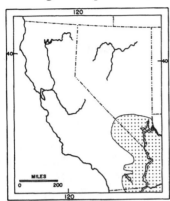

Golden-mantled ground squirrel

Spermophilus lateralis

Order Rodentia   **Family Sciuridae**

Identifying Features

These mountain-inhabiting ground squirrels with lateral stripes are commonly confused with chipmunks. They differ in that there is no stripe on the side of the head. They have a white stripe running from the shoulder to the hip on each side of the dark back. The short, bushy tail is gray to yellowish below and edged with white.

Measurements

Total length, 10.8 inches (275 mm); tail, 3.8 inches (95 mm); hind foot, 1.7 inches (43 mm); ear, 0.8 inch (20 mm); weight, 7 ounces (200 g).

Habitat

This species generally occurs in meadows or glades of evergreen forests in higher mountains.

Life Habits

These mammals feed during the daytime on buds, young leaves, flowers, seeds, berries, nuts, and fungi. Insects are also readily taken. Food is stored in the burrow. A litter of four to eight young is born in late spring. By early fall, both adults and young are fat and enter hibernation. At higher elevations, winter sleep may last for six months.

Golden-mantled
ground squirrel

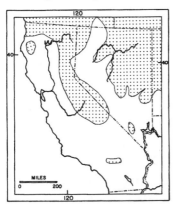

Sandy Truett

Western gray squirrel

Sciurus griseus

Order Rodentia   **Family Sciuridae**

Identifying Features

This tree squirrel is gray above. Many of the hairs have white tips. The belly is white. The tail is long and bushy.

Measurements

Total length, 22 inches (558 mm); tail, 10.5 inches (270 mm); hind foot, 3.2 inches (80 mm); ear, 1.2 inches (30 mm); weight, 1 pound (475 g).

Habitat

Along the coast, Western gray squirrels are restricted to oak woodlands. In the mountainous interior regions, they occur in both oak woodlands and redwood forests.

Life Habits

Western gray squirrels are active throughout the year. Most activity is in the early morning and late evening. During cold, stormy periods, they remain in the nest for days at a time. Food includes a range of plant materials including leaf buds, flowers, herbs, fungi, berries, pine cones, and acorns. These squirrels construct bulky nests of shredded bark and twigs high in trees. These are occupied in the summer. Most winter nests are in hollow trees. After a gestation period of about seven weeks, a litter of one to three young is born in the spring. While the young are in the nest, the female protects a territory surrounding the nest tree. *See related species 47 and 48.*

Western gray squirrel

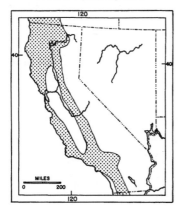

Douglas' squirrel

Tamiasciurus douglasii

Order Rodentia   **Family Sciuridae**

Identifying Features

This small tree squirrel has prominent black stripes, one on each side. Its tail is narrow and shorter than the head and body. Black-tipped hairs occur along the edge and on the tip of the tail. The dorsal coat color is dark reddish while the belly is yellowish. This squirrel is usually heard before it is seen.

Measurements

Total length, 12.8 inches (325 mm); tail, 4.9 inches (125 mm); hind foot, 1.9 inches (47 mm); ear, 1 inch (25 mm); weight, 8.1 ounces (250 g).

Habitat

Douglas squirrels are found in coniferous forests in northern and central California.

Life Habits

These squirrels are active throughout the year. In cold, stormy weather, they remain in their nests. They feed during the day. In summers, most activity is during mornings. Food includes fungi, nuts, and seeds. They often carry food to a "feeding stump" where they watch the surroundings as they extract the food from nuts or cones. After some time, a huge stack of debris accumulates there. Nests are in hollow trees or are built of twigs and bark high in the tree. Two litters of two to seven young are born, one litter in April or May and another as late as September.

Douglas' squirrel

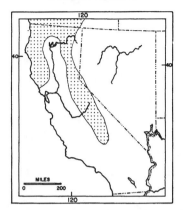

Northern flying squirrel

Glaucomys sabrinus

Order Rodentia   **Family Sciuridae**

Identifying Features

The combination of prominent fur-covered gliding membranes along the sides between the fore and hind legs, and soft silky fur is unique to flying squirrels. The ears are small and the bushy tail is broad and flattened. Dorsal color is brownish, the tail is blackish, and the belly is white to creamy white.

Measurements

Total length, 12.6 inches (320 mm); tail, 5.5 inches (140 mm); hind foot, 1.7 inches (43 mm); ear, 1.1 inches (28 mm); weight, 5.6 ounces (160 g).

Habitat

Flying squirrels are forest dwellers, being most common in dense coniferous areas.

Life Habits

Flying squirrels are the only North American members of the squirrel family that are not active during the day. As a result, they are rarely seen and little known by most people. They are active throughout the year. Their food consists of seeds, nuts, fungi, berries, insects, and even small birds. Nests are constructed of shredded bark in hollow trees. Sometimes they will build a roof over an abandoned bird nest and use it as a retreat. After a gestation period of 40 days, a litter of two to five young is born in May or June.

Northern flying squirrel

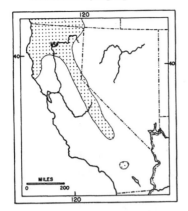

Northern pocket gopher

Thomomys talpoides

Order Rodentia   **Family Geomyidae**

Identifying Features

Rarely seen aboveground, this medium-sized rodent is modified for life in an underground burrow: the forefeet have elongated claws for digging, the ears are tiny, the wide head is flattened and wedge-shaped, the neck is short, the body is stout. Color is light in dry areas and almost black in moist regions.

Measurements

Total length, 9.5 inches (240 mm); tail, 3 inches (77 mm); hind foot, 1.3 inches (32 mm); ear, 0.4 inch (10 mm); weight, 6.7 ounces (190 g). Variation is plus or minus 25%. Pocket gophers that live in deep soils are usually larger.

Habitat

Pocket gophers occur mainly in soft soil. They are common in grasslands and meadows. Alfalfa fields are favored sites.

Life Habits

Gophers feed on vegetation, mostly in long feeding tunnels underground. Roots and bulbs are most commonly taken, but whole plants may be pulled into a burrow and eaten. A nest is built in a deep tunnel, often under a rock or the roots of a bush or tree. Generally there is only one gopher in a tunnel system that may have 20 or more earth mounds on the surface. Two to ten young per litter and one or two litters each year is normal. *See related species 49-51.*

Northern pocket gopher

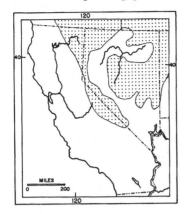

Little pocket mouse

Perognathus longimembris

Order Rodentia   **Family Heteromyidae**

Identifying Features

This small mouse has soft fur, a wide head, short neck and tiny ears. Its tail is not tufted and is longer than the head and body. Color is generally light pinkish buff above and white below. A well-developed fur-lined cheek pouch occurs on each side of the head.

Measurements

Total length, 5.1 inches (130 mm); tail, 2.1 inches (53 mm); hind foot, 0.7 inch (18 mm); ear, 0.2 inch (5 mm); weight, 0.3 ounce (9 g).

Habitat

These pocket mice are common in deserts and in sandy areas in desert grasslands.

Life Habits

Little pocket mice spend the winter in hibernation. They become active aboveground in late spring and disappear underground in early fall. They construct burrows under bushes. A burrow usually has three or four openings. These mice are active at night. They feed on the seeds of grasses and other small plants. Some insects and some green plants are eaten, especially in the spring. Usually seeds are collected and transported in the fur-lined cheek pouches to storage places in the burrows. A litter of three to six young is born after a gestation period of about four weeks. Two litters each summer are common. *See related species 52-55.*

Little pocket mouse

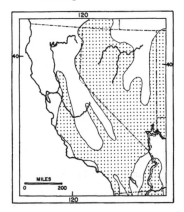

Spiny pocket mouse

Chaetodipus spinatus

Order Rodentia   **Family Heteromyidae**

Identifying Features

This is a larger version of the previous species. Its hair is harsh and its color is darker, usually a grayish buff above. The belly is whitish. It has distinct brown and light-colored spines on the rump. The tail is longer than the head and body and has a weakly developed tuft of hairs at the tip. Fur-lined cheek pouches are present.

Measurements

Total length, 8.2 inches (210 mm); tail, 4.5 inches (115 mm); hind foot, 1 inch (25 mm); ear, 0.4 inch (10 mm); weight, 0.9 ounce (25 g).

Habitat

These pocket mice are common inhabitants of sandy or gravelly soil in southeastern California. Most of the relatives of this species occur in desert situations.

Life Habits

Like other pocket mice, this species is strictly nocturnal. It is active from early spring to early fall and spends the cold months in hibernation. Their burrow is generally constructed under a bush or next to a rock. Food consists mostly of seeds, but green vegetation and insects are also eaten. Seeds are collected and stored in the burrow system. One or two litters (two to seven young) are born each year. *See related species 56-60.*

Spiny pocket mouse

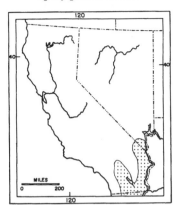

Ord's kangaroo rat

Dipodomys ordii

Order Rodentia   **Family Heteromyidae**

Identifying Features

Kangaroo rats are modified for jumping (saltatorial) locomotion. The hind legs and feet are enlarged. The forelimbs are small. The tail is long and has a well-developed tuft of hair at the tip. A white stripe runs across the thighs. The color of the back is generally tan, buff, or cinnamon. The belly has long, soft, white hairs. It also has fur-lined external cheek pouches.

Measurements

Total length, 10.0 inches (250 mm); tail, 5.9 inches (150 mm); hind foot, 1.5 inches (38 mm); ear, 0.5 inch (12 mm); weight, 1.6 ounces (44 g).

Habitat

Ord's kangaroo rats live mainly in open grasslands.

Life Habits

These nocturnal, seed-eating rodents store food in shallow holes in the ground or in their burrows. Various insects and newly sprouted seeds are also eaten. Kangaroo rats are active throughout the year. One to six, usually three, young are born in a litter. In the warmer parts of its range, this species has two litters in a year—one in the winter and one in the summer. *See related species 61-72.*

Ord's kangaroo rat

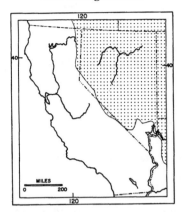

Dark kangaroo mouse

Microdipodops megacephalus

Order Rodentia   **Family Heteromyidae**

Identifying Features

This small, soft-haired rodent looks like a cross between a small kangaroo rat and a pocket mouse. Its head is large and wide and has fur-lined cheek pouches. The ears are small. The tail is relatively short, covered with short hairs, and has no tuft at the tip. The base of the tail is small, the middle is enlarged, and the tip is pointed. The soles of the feet are densely haired and edged with stiff, projecting hairs.

Measurements

Total length, 6.7 inches (170 mm); tail, 3.5 inches (90 mm); hind foot, 1 inch (25 mm); ear, 0.4 inch (10 mm); weight, 0.4 ounce (12 g).

Habitat

Dark kangaroo mice occur in loose, drifting sand and adjacent areas between 3900 (1190 m) and 7600 feet (2320 m) in northern and central Nevada and eastern California.

Life Habits

This species hibernates from late October to late March. Food consists of various seeds, insects, and green plants. Two litters of two to seven young (usually four) are born, one in the spring and one in the summer. During the active season, the day is spent in a burrow, the opening of which is plugged with loose soil. No food is stored in the burrow. *See related species 73.*

Dark kangaroo mouse

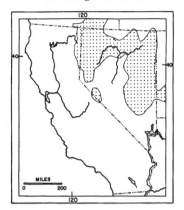

Beaver

Castor canadensis

Order Rodentia   **Family Castoridae**

Identifying Features
The large size and the adaptations for a life in and around water make the beaver quite distinct. It has webbed hind feet; a large, flattened, scale-covered tail; and small ears. The pelage is long, dense, and water repellant.

Measurements
Total length, 38 inches (980 mm); tail, 16 inches (406 mm); hind foot, 6.7 inches (170 mm); ear, 1.3 inches (32 mm); weight, 50 pounds (23 kg).

Habitat
Beaver live in or along permanent streams and lakes that are bordered by trees. In the desert, they occur along the Colorado River. They are now reduced in numbers and are exterminated in some areas.

Life Habits
These rodents generally live in family groups. Slapping the tail on water and other devices are used for communication. Beavers feed on the bark and outer layers of various bushes and trees, especially aspens, birches, and willows. They may build a dam of sticks, rocks, and mud across small streams, making a "beaver pond." They may also construct a dome-shaped lodge of sticks and mud that has an underwater entrance. In some places, "lodges" are constructed as burrows in stream banks. A litter of two to eight kits is born in April or May.

Beaver

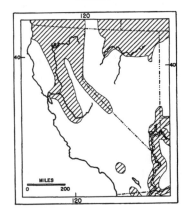

Western harvest mouse

Reithrodontomys megalotis

Order Rodentia   **Family Muridae**

Identifying Features

This small mouse has small ears; a long, slender, sparsely haired tail; and no external fur-lined cheek pouches. A vertical groove is present on the front of each upper incisor. It is brownish above, white below, and the sides have a line of buff-colored fur between the dorsal and ventral colors.

Measurements

Total length, 5.5 inches (140 mm); tail, 2.6 inches (65 mm); hind foot, 0.7 inch (18 mm); ear, 0.5 inch (12 mm); weight, 0.5 ounce (14 g).

Habitat

Harvest mice occur in grassy areas. They are most numerous in grasslands and mountain meadows.

Life Habits

These mice feed on seeds and plant growth. Most activity is at night, but they may feed during the day. Harvest mice are active throughout the year. They rest in a nest of grass at ground level or sometimes in a low bush. The nest is sometimes a modification of a bird's nest. The breeding season is April to October. After 23 days, a litter of one to seven helpless, hairless, and blind young is born. Two or more litters may be produced each summer. *See related species 74.*

Western harvest mouse

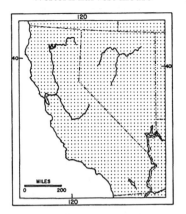

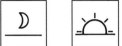

Deer mouse

Peromyscus maniculatus

Order Rodentia   **Family Muridae**

Identifying Features
Deer mice are similar to Harvest mice, but are larger, especially in ear length and tail diameter. There is no groove on the front surface of the upper incisor. Colors vary from dark grayish to a light buff brown above and white below. The tail is white with a narrow, distinct dark stripe on the dorsal surface. Young, like the young of most members of this family, are a light gray in their first coats of fur.

Measurements
Total length, 7.1 inches (180 mm); tail, 3.2 inches (80 mm); hind foot, 0.9 inch (22 mm); ear, 0.7 inch (18 mm); weight, 1 ounce (28 g).

Habitat
These mice are most common in grasslands, but some live in small grassy areas surrounded by dense forests. Related species occur in almost all habitats in the area.

Life Habits
Deer mice are active at night throughout the year. They construct short underground burrows with a nest of grasses or other soft material. Their diet includes insects and other arthropods, but is mainly fungi, berries, fruits, small nuts, and seeds. After a gestation of 28 days, a litter of three to seven young is born. *See related species 75-79.*

Deer mouse

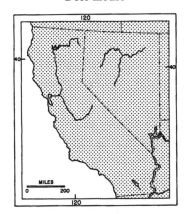

Northern grasshopper mouse

Onychomys leucogaster

Order Rodentia   **Family Muridae**

Identifying Features
This plump-bodied mouse has a short, thick tail and relatively short legs. The tail, less than half the length of the head and body, is thick and constricted at the base. The back is generally pale cinnamon to light brown. The belly and feet are white.

Measurements
Total length, 5.4 inches (138 mm); tail, 1.6 inches (40 mm); hind foot, 0.8 inch (20 mm); ear, 0.8 inch (20 mm); weight, 1.2 ounces (35 g).

Habitat
Grasshopper mice are dwellers of sandy, vegetated areas in the desert and desert grasslands.

Life Habits
This species, active at night throughout the year, is more of a carnivore than other small rodents. Food consists mainly of invertebrates, especially grasshoppers. They hunt in small groups and have a high-pitched whistle that apparently helps keep the group together. Each group has a system of burrows: a central nest burrow (closed during the day), food storage burrows (seeds for use when insects are not available), and a series of short escape burrows throughout the normal hunting territory. A litter of four to five naked, blind young is born after a gestation period of 30 to 45 days. Two litters per year are common. *See related species 80.*

Northern grasshopper mouse

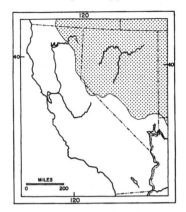

Hispid cotton rat

Sigmodon hispidus

Order Rodentia   **Family Muridae**

Identifying Features

This species is the size of a small rat. The coat is coarsely grizzled, generally blackish or brownish mixed with buff or gray. The sides and belly are lighter than the back. The tail is shorter than the head and body.

Measurements

Total length, 9.8 inches (248 mm); tail, 4.1 inches (105 mm); hind foot, 1.3 inches (32 mm); ear, 0.7 inch (18 mm); weight, 3.2 ounces (85 g).

Habitat

In this area, cotton rats occur only in tall grasses and weed-grown fields along the lower Colorado River.

Life Habits

This species, active throughout the year, often feeds during the day. They have cleared runways along which are often found small stacks of short pieces of grass stems. Food is mainly the stems and new growth of grasses and weeds. Their nest, constructed of grasses, is under piles of dead vegetation or even in abandoned Pocket gopher burrows. After a gestation period of four weeks, a litter of two to ten blind, naked young is born. One female may have as many as nine litters in one year. Some may be born during almost every month, but most are born between June and October. *See related species 81.*

Hispid cotton rat

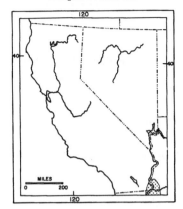

Bushy-tailed woodrat

Neotoma cinerea

Order Rodentia   **Family Muridae**

Identifying Features

This large woodrat is thickly furred and has a bushy squirrellike tail that is shorter than the head and body. Its ears are large and are bare on the tips. The coat is soft, dark above and white on the belly.

Measurements

Total length, 15.6 inches (400 mm); tail, 5.1 inches (130 mm); hind foot, 1.7 inches (43 mm); ear, 1.4 inches (35 mm); weight, 10.6 ounces (300 g).

Habitat

This species occurs at the forest edge, often near rock ledges, and sometimes in caves, mines, or abandoned buildings.

Life Habits

These nocturnal rats are active throughout the year. Food includes fungi and a wide variety of herbs, including stems and leaf shoots of trees. Some insects are also eaten. They build a den that may be only a grass-lined nest under a few sticks in a rock crevice to a large heap of sticks and other debris in open areas. Two litters (March and May) are common, each with two to four young. They are sometimes called Pack rats or Trade rats because they often drop whatever they happen to be carrying back to the den and pick up some bright object such as a spoon or ring. *See related species 82-84.*

Bushy-tailed woodrat

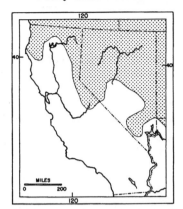

Western red-backed vole

Clethrionomys californicus

Order Rodentia   **Family Muridae**

Identifying Features

This small, chunky mouse has a short tail and short ears. Its coat consists of long, grizzled hairs. A broad dorsal stripe ranges in color from bright chestnut to yellowish brown.

Measurements

Total length, 5.9 inches (150 mm); tail, 2 inches (50 mm); hind foot, 0.8 inch (20 mm); ear, 0.5 inch (12 mm); weight, 1 ounce (28 g).

Habitat

These voles are most common in forested mountains above 8000 feet (2440 m), usually near or under decaying logs.

Life Habits

These mice are active throughout the year. Their activities are not restricted to the night. During winter, they construct feeding tunnels under the snow. Food is almost entirely vegetation. A fungus (*Endogone*) that grows on decaying leaves and wood makes up all of the food of some individuals. Sprouting seeds are also eaten. Three to eight (usually four) young are born in a litter and more than one litter per summer is common. The nest is usually only a small pile of soft vegetation under a log or in a burrow under a root.

Western red-backed vole

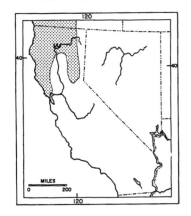

Heather vole

Phenacomys intermedius

Order Rodentia   **Family Muridae**

Identifying Features

This is a chunky, short-snouted mouse with short ears; large, beadlike eyes; and long, loose, soft, grizzled pelage. It looks much like the preceding species, but lacks the rusty or reddish stripe down the back and its short tail is sharply bicolored—dark above and white below. The feet are white.

Measurements

Total length, 5.5 inches (140 mm); tail, 1.4 inches (35 mm); hind foot, 0.8 inch (20 mm); ear, 0.6 inch (15 mm); weight, 1.3 ounces (37 g).

Habitat

Heather voles are not common anywhere. They live in high mountain grassy and heather patches near water. In this region, they occur in the Blue Mountains of northern California and in the higher areas of Yosemite National Park.

Life Habits

Voles are active in early evenings and at night throughout the year. In the winter, they construct nests of soft grasses and lichens aboveground under snow. At other times, the nest is underground. Food includes lichens, green plants, berries, and tree bark. After 21 days, a litter of two to eight blind, naked, and helpless young is born. One female may have three litters in a year. *See related species 85 and 86.*

Heather vole

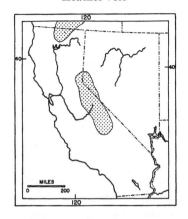

Long-tailed vole

Microtus longicaudus

Order Rodentia   **Family Muridae**

Identifying Features

At first glance, this looks like either of the two preceding species. It is a chunky, short-snouted mouse with short ears; large, bead-like eyes; and long, loose, grizzled hair. It differs in being darker colored, brownish gray above, and having dark feet. Its habitat (dense grass) and habit of constructing narrow runways through dense grass that often are sunk into the ground, is usually enough to distinguish this species.

Measurements

Total length, 7.2 inches (185 mm); tail, 2.4 inches (62 mm); hind foot, 0.8 inch (20 mm); ear, 0.5 inch (12 mm); weight, 1.6 ounces (44 g).

Habitat

These voles live in grasslands and open grassy meadows, from 4300 to over 11,000 feet. They live in well-developed runways among the roots of grasses or in ground litter.

Life Habits

Voles are active throughout the year. Food is green vegetation. Roots, stems, and leaves are all eaten. A nest of grass is built aboveground. In a single year, a female may give birth to as many as ten litters, each with two to eight blind, naked young. *See related species 87-90.*

Long-tailed vole

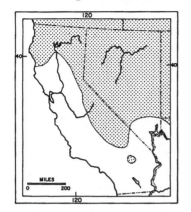

Sagebrush vole

Lagurus curtatus

Order Rodentia   **Family Muridae**

Identifying Features

Like the preceding three species, this vole is chunky and short-snouted. It also has short ears; large beadlike eyes; short tail; and long, loose, grizzled pelage. Its pale color (ash gray), white belly and feet, and short tail (less than 1 inch—25 mm) make it unique in this area. It alone of the voles has ears that are more than half the length of the hind foot.

Measurements

Total length, 4.8 inches (122 mm); tail, 0.9 inch (22 mm); hind foot, 0.6 inch (15 mm); ear, 0.4 inch (10 mm); weight, 1 ounce (28 g).

Habitat

As indicated by the common name, this vole is almost always found in dry sagebrush areas, usually on slopes above the valley floor. In this region, it is known only from northern areas.

Life Habits

Sagebrush voles are active throughout the year, both during the day and at night. In the open sagebrush areas where they live, trails are poorly defined. Piles of droppings often are the best indication of their presence. Food consists of almost anything that is green. A litter of four to eight young is born in a grass-lined nest in a short, shallow, underground burrow. More than one litter each year is common.

Sagebrush vole

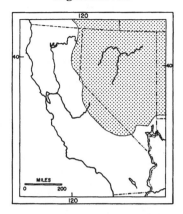

Muskrat

Ondatra zibethicus

Order Rodentia   **Family Muridae**

Identifying Features

This large rodent is adapted for living in and near water. The tail
is scaly, laterally compressed, and about the length of the head
and body. The toes of the hind feet are fringed with stiff hairs that
aid in swimming.

Measurements

Total length, 20 inches (500 mm); tail, 10 inches (250 mm); hind
foot, 2.8 inches (72 mm); ear, 0.8 inch (20 mm); weight, 4 pounds
(1.8 kg).

Habitat

Muskrats live in and around permanent streams, lakes, and ponds
through most of this area, even up to elevations of 11,000 feet
(3354 m).

Life Habits

Muskrats, active at night throughout the year, eat any plant that
grows in or near water. They also eat crops such as corn, when
available. Dens are constructed as domed structures of vegetation
and mud that rise above the water and have an entrance below
water. At times, dens are dug in the banks of streams or lakes,
utilizing underwater entrances. One to 11 (usually six) young are
born in a litter. At high elevations and in the north, two litters are
common; while at low elevations in the south, three or four litters
may be produced.

Muskrat

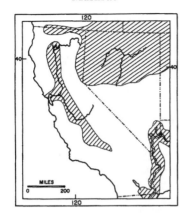

Norway rat

Rattus norvegicus

Order Rodentia   **Family Muridae**

Identifying Features

This rat resembles the Woodrat in general size, but differs in having short ears and a sparsely haired, scaly tail that is slightly shorter than the head and body. The back, belly, and feet are grayish, with some brownish tones on the back.

Measurements

Total length, 14.6 inches (370 mm); tail, 6.7 inches (170 mm); hind foot, 1.4 inches (35 mm); ear, 0.9 inch (22 mm); weight, 10 ounces (280 g).

Habitat

This rat is rarely found in undisturbed natural situations but occurs in buildings, trash heaps, city dumps, and other places that have been modified by humans.

Life Habits

This native of the Old World lives with humans throughout most of the world. Norway rats eat a wide variety of crops and stores of animal and human foods. Its reproductive rate is high. A litter has two to 20 young, and up to nine litters are born in one year. Adulthood is reached in 90 to 120 days. These rats are carriers of a series of diseases including plague, typhus, and spotted fever. The white and hooded rats of the pet store and the laboratory are special varieties of this species. *See related species 91.*

Norway rat

House mouse

Mus musculus

Order Rodentia   **Family Muridae**

Identifying Features

This mouse is about the same size and shape as the Western harvest mouse, but its tail is long, scaly, hairless, and is gray both above and below. The belly is usually grayish, but sometimes has a whitish or buff wash. The upper incisors are not grooved, but do have a distinctive notch in the grinding surface when viewed from the side.

Measurements

Total length, 6.7 inches (170 mm); tail, 3.1 inches (80 mm); hind foot, 0.7 inch (18 mm); ear, 0.5 inch (12 mm); weight, 0.7 ounce (20 g).

Habitat

This mouse is rarely found in undisturbed natural situations, but is generally in and around buildings and agricultural areas.

Life Habits

Like the Norway rat, the House mouse is a native of the Old World that has also adapted to living with man throughout most of the world. They eat a wide variety of food including crops, stored animal and human food, as well as insects. When food is available, they are capable of producing several litters (up to 14) of up to 16 young in a year. Nests are of soft material in hidden places such as holes in the ground, in walls, or under boards.

100

House mouse

Western jumping mouse

Zapus princeps

Order Rodentia   **Family Dipodidae**

Identifying Features
This is a rather large mouse that has large hind feet, enlarged hind legs, and an elongated tail. It is adapted for leaping (saltatorial) locomotion. The upper incisors are grooved on the front surface. The back is dark, the sides yellowish or buff, the belly white. The ears are short and edged with light hairs.

Measurements
Total length, 9.5 inches (240 mm); tail, 5.7 inches (145 mm); hind foot, 1.3 inches (32 mm); ear, 0.6 inch (15 mm); weight, 0.8 ounce (23 g).

Habitat
This species occurs mainly in mountains between 4000 and 11,000 feet (1220-3354 m), especially under aspens and willows.

Life Habits
Jumping mice are active during the night in the warmer parts of the year. They hibernate during the cold months. Food consists of insects, fungi, and a series of berries and seeds. They become very fat in the fall, some gaining almost 25% of their body weight in three weeks before entering hibernation. A litter of two to seven young is born early in the summer. Nests are grass-lined structures in underground burrows. *See related species 92.*

Western jumping mouse

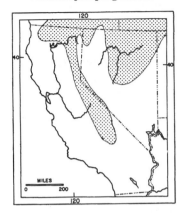

Porcupine

Erethizon dorsatum

Order Rodentia   **Family Erethizontidae**

Identifying Features

This large rodent (larger than a small dog) has specialized hair in the form of spines (quills) on the back, sides, and tail. It is chunky-bodied and has short legs. The claws (four front, five behind) are long and curved.

Measurements

Total length, 35 inches (890 mm); tail, 8.2 inches (210 mm); hind foot, 4.3 inches (108 mm); ear, 1.2 inches (30 mm); weight, 18 pounds (8.2 kg).

Habitat

Porcupines are most common in evergreen forests; however, in this area, they are found almost anywhere there are trees, from sea level to above timberline.

Life Habits

Porcupines are active throughout the year, generally at night. They feed on a variety of plants. Most noticeable is the bark that is stripped from the trunks and branches of trees, especially in the winter. Twigs, leaves, stems of various trees, and herbs are also eaten. Porcupines are usually solitary and have a den in a cave, crevice, or hollow tree. After a gestation period of about 120 days, a single young (sometimes twins) is born, usually in late spring.

Porcupine

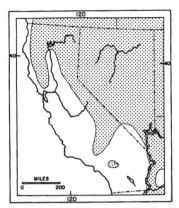

Sandy Truett

Coyote

Canis latrans

Order Carnivora   **Family Canidae**

Identifying Features

The Coyote looks very much like a small German shepherd dog. It is buff gray or grizzled above, buff below, and has a black-tipped tail.

Measurements

Total length, 47 inches (1.2 m); tail, 14 inches (350 mm); hind foot, 8.0 inches (200 mm); ear, 4.4 inches (110 mm); weight, 23 pounds (10.5 kg).

Habitat

Coyotes occur from high mountains to low deserts. They are often common on rangelands and in the suburbs of towns and cities.

Life Habits

Coyotes are usually most active in early morning and late afternoon throughout the year. Some are active at night and on cooler overcast days. They have been reported as the best runners among the wild dogs. They can run for long distances at about 25 miles per hour and can dash up to 40 mph. Food consists of a wide range of animal and vegetable matter. Rodents, rabbits, and insects as well as juniper berries, cactus fruit, and berries are commonly eaten. Some deer and domestic livestock are killed by coyotes, but most eaten by them had died of other causes and were eaten as carrion. During the spring, a litter of up to 11 pups is born in an underground den.

Coyote

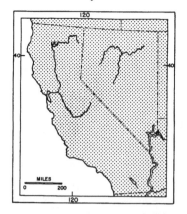

Gray wolf

Canis lupus

Order Carnivora   **Family Canidae**

Identifying Features

A small wolf is similar to a large coyote or a very large German shepherd dog. Even experts are sometimes uncertain of sight identifications. Coat color varies from light buff to almost black. Differences include the nose pad being 1 inch (25 mm) or more wide (smaller in coyotes and dogs) and the tail held out behind when running (between the legs in a coyote).

Measurements

Total length, 78 inches (2 m); tail, 18 inches (450 mm); hind foot, 12 inches (300 mm); ear, 4 inches (100 mm); weight, 110 pounds (50 kg). Males are 20% larger than females.

Habitat

The wolf formerly occurred in most of Nevada and the mountainous parts of eastern California. It is now probably exterminated. The last sightings were in 1920, in the Sierra Nevada Mountains.

Life Habits

Generally wolves lived in small family groups consisting of an adult female, her mate, and the young of the year, and perhaps the young of her previous litter. Members of the group often joined in a "wolf pack" for hunting. The annual hunting range of such a group was as much as 50 miles (80 km) in length and perhaps as wide. Timber wolf and Lobo are other names.

Gray wolf
(dots = former range,
lines = present range)

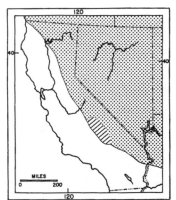

Sandy Truett

Red fox

Vulpes vulpes

Order Carnivora   **Family Canidae**

Identifying Features
This dog-shaped carnivore has long, pointed ears; a long muzzle; and a very bushy, white-tipped tail. Dorsal color is usually a reddish yellow shade. The feet are black.

Measurements
Total length, 43 inches (1.1 m); tail, 17 inches (430 mm); hind foot, 6.7 inches (170 mm); ear, 3.3 inches (84 mm); weight, 10 pounds (4.5 kg).

Habitat
Red foxes live in forests, brush, and agricultural regions in the central and the coastal regions of California as well as in the Sierra Nevada Mountains of northeastern California and west-central Nevada. In California, under the name "Sierra Nevada red fox" (*Vulpes vulpes necator*), they are listed by California Game and Fish as a "rare" mammal.

Life Habits
These foxes are active throughout the year, mostly in the early evening and at night. Food consists of insects and small rodents. Occasionally a rabbit is taken as are some fruits and berries. They generally live in burrows or in a rock crevice. The same den is often occupied by generation after generation of foxes. A litter of one to eight pups is born in late spring or early summer. The female, male, and young live and hunt as a family unit until the young leave the following year.

Red fox

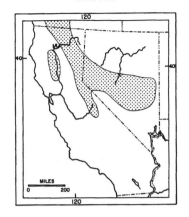

Kit fox

Vulpes macrotis

Order Carnivora   **Family Canidae**

Identifying Features
The Kit fox looks much like a small, light-colored Red fox with unusually large ears. It is the smallest fox in the Americas. The back is a yellowish gray, the underparts white, the tail is black-tipped, and the feet and ears are buff.

Measurements
Total length, 31 inches (790 mm); tail, 10 inches (250 mm); hind foot, 5 inches (125 mm); ear, 3.3 inches (84 mm); weight, 4.4 pounds (2 kg). The females are slightly smaller than the males.

Habitat
Kit foxes live in deserts and desert grasslands as well as in the San Joaquin valley and adjacent coastal range valleys. Much of their distribution coincides with that of the larger species of kangaroo rats.

Life Habits
Kit foxes are active at night throughout the year. Their underground burrow usually has three or four escape tunnels. Food includes kangaroo rats, pocket mice, some rabbits, and some insects. A litter of four to five young is born in March or April. Populations known as the San Joaquin kit fox (*Vulpes macrotis mutica*) are listed by California as "rare" mammals and by the U.S. Fish and Wildlife Service as an "endangered species."

Kit fox

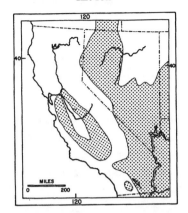

Gray fox

Urocyon cinereoargenteus

Order Carnivora   **Family Canidae**

Identifying Features

This fox is similar to the Red fox, but is darker in color, has a tail that is larger, a dorsal stripe of stiff black hairs, and is tipped with black. The color of the back ranges from grizzled grayish to reddish. The throat is white and the chest, sides, and belly are reddish.

Measurements

Total length, 37 inches (940 mm); tail, 17 inches (430 mm); hind foot, 5.3 inches (135 mm); ear, 2.6 inches (65 mm); weight, 8.4 pounds (3.8 kg). Females are smaller than males.

Habitat

Gray foxes occur in deserts, open forests, and brush from sea level to 9000 feet (2750 m).

Life Habits

Habits of the Gray foxes are similar to those of the other foxes. They are more secretive than other species. Almost all of their activity is at night. Food consists of a mixture of plant and animal materials. Juniper berries, fruits, acorns, insects, birds, and especially small mammals are included in their diet. This species can climb trees to get to food or to escape an enemy. It has a den in a hollow log, under a boulder, or in a rock crevice. A litter of two to five young is born in the spring. *See related species 93.*

Gray fox

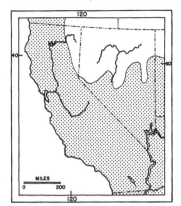

Black bear

Ursus americanus

Order Carnivora   **Family Ursidae**

Identifying Features

This large, heavily-built, short-tailed carnivore is usually black in color, above and below. Some are cinnamon; others are almost tan. The feet are short and broad.

Measurements

Total length, 63 inches (1.6 m); tail, 3.5 inches (90 mm); hind foot, 9.5 inches (240 mm); ear, 5 inches (125 mm); weight, 250 pounds (120 kg). Females are smaller than the males. Sometimes old males reach weights of about 500 pounds.

Habitat

Bears are mostly restricted to forested and wooded areas, especially at intermediate elevations. Now absent in cultivated areas, they are locally more common than they were 100 years ago.

Life Habits

Bears are most active at night but sometimes are active even in the middle of the day. During cold periods, they spend most of their time sleeping. They have a den in a hollow tree, rock crevice, or hole in the ground. Bears are omnivorous, feeding on a wide range of plant and animal material. Fruits, berries, acorns, plant shoots, roots, bulbs, fish, insects, rodents, rabbits—all are eaten. One to four cubs are born in late winter. The young are small (about 1.5 pounds—0.7 kg), blind, and helpless at birth.

Black bear

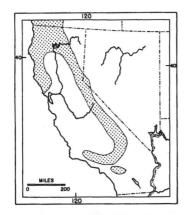

Grizzly bear

Ursus arctos

Order Carnivora   **Family Ursidae**

Identifying Features

The Grizzly bear is larger than the Black bear. It is a yellowish brown to black in dorsal color and has a prominent hump at the shoulders.

Measurements

Total length, 85 inches (2.1 m); tail, 4 inches (100 mm); hind foot, 12 inches (300 mm); ear, 5 inches (125 mm); weight, 900 pounds (400 kg).

Habitat

Grizzly bears formerly lived in mountains and along major streams in the lowlands of both states. They were exterminated in California by 1922. None have been recorded from Nevada in historic times.

Life Habits

Habits of these bears are similar to those of Black bears. Food consists of almost any edible material. Dead animals are fed upon as is garbage and food in campgrounds. They have a larger feeding territory (up to 25 miles in diameter) than the Black bear. After a gestation period of about 180 days, two or three, tiny, almost hairless, blind cubs are born. Adult size is reached in the third year. In captivity, they live for as long as 34 years. Under the name "California Golden Bear," it is the official symbol of California and appears on flags, uniform patches, and other state insignia.

Grizzly bear
(former range)

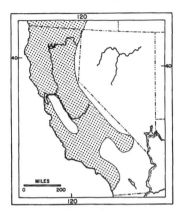

Ringtail

Bassariscus astutus

Order Carnivora **Family Procyonidae**

Identifying Features

This is a small-bodied, long-tailed carnivore that is somewhat catlike in general form. The tail has alternating bands, eight black and eight white. The tip of the tail is black. The back is a yellowish gray, the belly is whitish.

Measurements

Total length, 31 inches (790 mm); tail, 15 inches (380 mm); hind foot, 3 inches (75 mm); ear, 2 inches (50 mm); weight, 2.2 pounds (1 kg).

Habitat

Ringtails generally live in areas of rock exposures, commonly in rocky canyons below 6000 feet (1830 m) in elevation.

Life Habits

Ringtails are active throughout the year, almost entirely at night. They feed mainly on small rodents, especially woodrats and other species that also live in rocky situations. Lizards, birds, insects, and other invertebrates are also taken. In season, they eat various fruits and berries. Their den can be in a rock crevice, shallow cave, hollow tree, or even abandoned buildings. After a gestation period of about 53 days, a litter of two to four blind, fuzzy young are born in May or June. Ringtails live up to eight years in captivity.

Ringtail

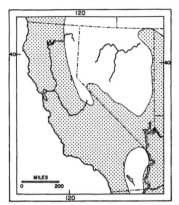

Raccoon

Procyon lotor

Order Carnivora   **Family Procyonidae**

Identifying Features

The Raccoon is a stout-bodied carnivore with a ringed, bushy tail somewhat resembling that of the Ringtail. The face has a well-developed dark mask around the eyes. The back is a mixture of dark and light-colored hairs. The black-tipped tail has five to seven black rings alternating with rings of yellowish white hairs.

Measurements

Total length, 30 inches (760 mm); tail, 11 inches (280 mm); hind foot, 4.7 inches (120 mm); ear, 2.2 inches (55 mm); weight, 22 pounds (10 kg). Some old, fat males weigh as much as 40 pounds.

Habitat

Raccoons are common in areas of permanent water, along streams and irrigation canals, generally at elevations below 6000 feet (1830 m).

Life Habits

Raccoons are active throughout the year, mostly after dark. Much of their food is taken along streams and includes fish, frogs, invertebrates, birds, mice, and a range of vegetable material. Grains, fruits, and melons are all eaten when available. One to six (usually four) blind, helpless young are born in April or May in a den hidden under a boulder, in a hollow tree, or similar place.

Raccoon

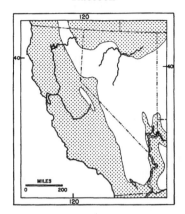

Marten

Martes americana

Order Carnivora   **Family Mustelidae**

Identifying Features

The Marten is a long-bodied, short-legged carnivore with catlike ears. It is the size of a large tree squirrel. The back is a golden brown color, the throat and chest are yellowish. The belly is slightly paler than the back. The fur is dense, soft, and in high demand for fur coats. The feet and tip of the tail are black.

Measurements

Total length, 25.5 inches (650 mm); tail, 8.2 inches (210 mm); hind foot, 3.3 inches (84 mm); ear, 1.6 inches (40 mm); weight, 2 pounds (0.9 kg). The females are as much as 25% smaller than the males.

Habitat

Martens are forest dwellers, occurring most commonly at high elevations in dense forests of fir and spruce.

Life Habits

Martens are active throughout the year, generally at night. They feed in trees as well as on the ground. Food consists of small mammals (especially Red squirrels), birds, insects, and some fruits and berries. They usually have a den in a hollow log or hollow tree but sometimes rest in the branches of a tree. Up to five blind, helpless young are born in a litter, usually in April. In captivity, a marten has lived for 17 years. *See related species 94.*

Marten

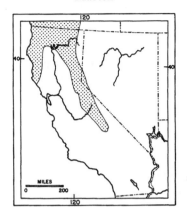

Long-tailed weasel

Mustela frenata

Order Carnivora   **Family Mustelidae**

Identifying Features

The weasel shape is well-known: small, short-legged, and long-bodied. The Long-tailed weasel has a black-tipped tail that is about half the length of the head and body. The back is brownish in color, the belly is yellowish white. During winter in the northern part of this area, the color is white except for the black tip of the tail.

Measurements

Total length, 16 inches (406 mm); tail, 5 inches (125 mm); hind foot, 2 inches (50 mm); ear, 0.8 inch (20 mm); weight, 9.5 ounces (270 g). The males are larger and almost twice the weight of the females.

Habitat

Long-tailed weasels occur from low grasslands to high mountains. They are usually near water.

Life Habits

These weasels are active throughout the year, mainly at night. Most activity is on the ground and in underground burrows of other animals. They sometimes climb trees to reach food. Their den, often a nest originally built by some other mammal, is usually under a pile of rocks or under a tree stump. They feed on small rodents, and to a lesser extent, on birds and bird eggs. A litter (usually five) of blind, helpless young is born in mid-April.

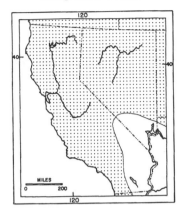

Long-tailed weasel

Ermine

Mustela erminea

Order Carnivora   **Family Mustelidae**

Identifying Features

This is the smallest carnivore in the area. It has the typical weasel shape: short-legged, long-bodied, and short-eared. Its black-tipped tail is only about a third of the length of the head and body. The color is brown above, whitish below. Like the Long-tailed weasel, its color in winter is white except for the black-tipped tail.

Measurements

Total length, 10 inches (250 mm); tail, 2.4 inches (62 mm); hind foot, 1.2 inches (30 mm); ear, 0.6 inch (15 mm); weight, 1.8 ounces (50 g). Females are smaller than the males.

Habitat

Ermines occur in a wide variety of situations, especially along bushy streams, in fence rows, and on rocky hillsides. They do not occur in the low deserts.

Life Habits

Ermines are active throughout the year, mainly at night. They feed entirely on small animals, especially mice. Lizards, birds, rats, and even small rabbits are killed and eaten. Their den is in a burrow, usually under a fallen tree, boulder, or other protected situation. A litter of four to eight blind, helpless young is born in the spring. The male helps in feeding the young by bringing food to the den.

Ermine

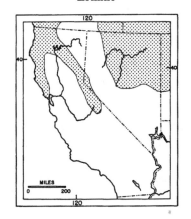

Mink

Mustela vison

Order Carnivora   **Family Mustelidae**

Identifying Features

This large weasel has dense, water-repellant fur. The color is dark brown, darkest on the tip of the tail and on the middle of the back. The tail is about half of the length of the head and body. Unlike other weasels, its belly is dark. A white chin patch is usually present.

Measurements

Total length, 24 inches (610 mm); tail, 7 inches (180 mm); hind foot, 2.8 inches (72 mm); ear, 0.6 inch (15 mm); weight, 2.2 pounds (1 kg). Females are about 10% smaller and weigh up to 50% less than males.

Habitat

Mink are restricted to lakes and streams in northern California and Nevada at elevations below 9000 feet (2750 m).

Life Habits

Mink are active throughout the year, mainly at night. They are seldom seen far from water. Their dens are usually in a hole in a river bank, but may be an abandoned muskrat or beaver lodge. They are generally solitary and often move from place to place in a territory that may extend a mile along a stream. Food consists of frogs, fish, crayfish, muskrats, and other aquatic animals. A litter (usually two to six) of blind, helpless young is born in April or May. Their skin is in great demand in the fur trade.

Mink

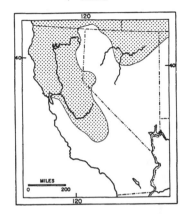

Wolverine

Gulo gulo

Order Carnivora   **Family Mustelidae**

Identifying Features

This large, chunky carnivore looks like a small bear with a bushy tail. It is dark brown, almost blackish, on the back. The head is grayish. Wide light stripes run from the shoulder down each side and meet on the rump. The throat and belly have yellowish white spots. The soles of the feet are naked in summer, heavily haired in winter.

Measurements

Total length, 42 inches (1.05 m); tail, 9 inches (228 mm); hind foot, 7.2 inches (185 mm); ear, 1.2 inches (30 mm); weight, 50 pounds (23 kg). Females are about 10% smaller in length and 30% less in weight than the males.

Habitat

Wolverines live in forested areas. Probably never common, they now occur only in remote northern areas. Listed by California as a "rare" mammal.

Life Habits

Wolverines are active throughout the year, both day and night. One male may defend a hunting territory of 100 square miles. Two or three females may live in this territory. Wolverines eat almost anything, animal or vegetable. They eat dead animals (carrion) as well as killing things as large as an elk. Two or three young are born in the spring.

Wolverine
(lines = former range, dots = present range)

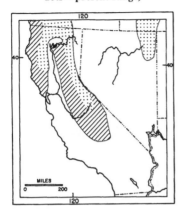

Badger

Taxidea taxus

Order Carnivora   **Family Mustelidae**

Identifying Features
This stout-bodied carnivore is well-adapted for burrowing. The legs, neck, tail, and ears are short. The forefeet have long, strong claws useful in digging. The head is broad and triangular. Color is black on the head, white on the cheeks, and a wide line down the back. The back and sides are a mixture of black and white hairs.

Measurements
Total length, 31 inches (780 mm); tail, 5.1 inches (130 mm); hind foot, 4.4 inches (110 mm); ear, 2 inches (50 mm); weight, 20 pounds (9 kg).

Habitat
Badgers live in a variety of nonforested areas from high mountains to low deserts throughout the area.

Life Habits
Badgers are active throughout the year, mainly in late afternoon or at night. They tend to be solitary. Food consists mostly of small rodents, reptiles, and insects that are usually dug from the ground. During much of the year, badgers dig new burrows each morning for a day retreat. In the spring, females dig a deep burrow and line it with grasses. There one to five (usually two) young are born in March or April. During cold winter periods, Badgers sleep for days at a time, living on fat.

Badger

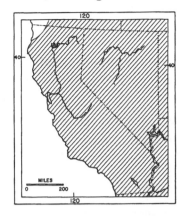

Spotted skunk

Spilogale gracilis

Order Carnivora   **Family Mustelidae**

Identifying Features

This small skunk (kitten-sized) is black with white spots, one on the forehead, one below each ear, and others variously scattered over the back and sides. The bushy tail is tipped with white.

Measurements

Total length, 17 inches (430 mm); tail, 6 inches (150 mm); hind foot, 1.8 inches (45 mm); ear, 0.8 inch (20 mm); weight, 1.2 pounds (500 g).

Habitat

Spotted skunks live below 8000 feet (2440 m) in hilly or rough, broken country. In deserts, they occur near water sources.

Life Habits

These small skunks are active at night during most of the year. In cold periods, they may stay in a den for days. Often winter dens are communal, with two or more skunks present. Food is mainly insects and other invertebrates although small lizards, rodents, fruit, and berries are eaten. A litter of two to ten (usually four) young is born in March or April. By late summer, the young accompany their mother on her nightly hunting trips. When alarmed, Spotted skunks have an unusual "handstand" reaction that results in a spectacular display of the back and tail. If the warning is unheeded, the provoker may then be sprayed from the anal scent glands.

Spotted skunk

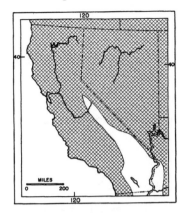

Striped skunk

Mephitis mephitis

Order Carnivora   **Family Mustelidae**

Identifying Features
This is a black, cat-sized carnivore that has white markings on the head, neck, shoulders, back, and on part of the large bushy tail. The legs are short; the movements deliberate.

Measurements
Total length, 28 inches (700 mm); tail, 12 inches (300 mm); hind foot, 3 inches (77 mm); ear, 1.1 inches (28 mm); weight, 6.6 pounds (3 kg). In the fall, an old, fat male may weigh up to 15 pounds (6.8 kg).

Habitat
Striped skunks live in more-or-less open country in woodlands, brush areas, and grasslands, usually near water. They are absent from much of the Great Basin Desert and Death Valley.

Life Habits
These skunks are active at night throughout the year. During cold periods, they may remain in a den for days. They feed on both plant and animal material including various fruits, bird eggs, insects, worms, as well as other invertebrates. Dead animals (carrion) are a major source of food. A litter of four to ten (generally five) blind, helpless young is born in May or June. By the end of summer, the young follow their mother on hunting trips. Dens are in holes in the ground, sometimes under a rock or a building. These skunks can live up to six years in captivity.

Striped skunk

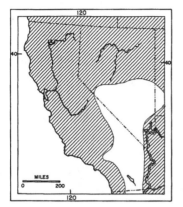

River otter

Lutra canadensis

Order Carnivora   **Family Mustelidae**

Identifying Features

This large carnivore is well-adapted for a life in and around water.
The body is somewhat teardrop in shape; the ears are small. The
tail is thick at the base and becomes smaller toward the tip. The
toes are webbed and can be broadly spread. The hair is dense and
waterproof. The back is brownish, the belly is paler.

Measurements

Total length, 51 inches (1.3 m); tail, 32 inches (820 mm); hind
foot, 5.9 inches (150 mm); ear, 2 inches (50 mm); weight, 20
pounds (9 kg).

Habitat

River otters once occurred throughout this area, wherever there
were permanent streams. Recent observations have been along the
lower Colorado River and in northern California.

Life Habits

River otters are active throughout the year, mainly at night.
Almost all activity is in rivers and streams or along the adjacent
river bank. Their den is a hole in the bank, often under the roots
of a tree from which the soil has been washed away. River otters
are generally solitary. Food is mainly fish, but invertebrates,
frogs, and some birds are also eaten. A litter of two to five young
is born in the spring.

River otter

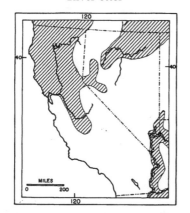

Jaguar

Felis onca

Order Carnivora   **Family Felidae**

Identifying Features

This is a large spotted cat that is about the size of the Old World Leopard. The tail is spotted, not striped. Some black (melanistic) individuals have been reported.

Measurements

Total length, 90 inches (2.3 m); tail, 26 inches (650 mm); hind foot, 10.8 inches (275 mm); weight, 285 pounds (130 kg). Females are 15% smaller than the males.

Habitat

Jaguars formerly occurred in the desert grasslands and lower mountains of southern California, but have been exterminated for several decades.

Life Habits

Jaguars are solitary animals that are usually active at night. As is true of most large carnivores, these cats require a large hunting range, perhaps covering 100 to 200 square miles (up to 500 square kilometers) in a year. Food consists of various large animals, especially deer, and some domestic animals may be killed. Along rivers, Jaguars scoop fish from the water. Two to four kittens are born in a litter after a gestation period of 100 days. They survive up to 22 years in captivity.

Jaguar
(former range)

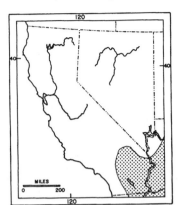

Mountain lion

Felis concolor

Order Carnivora   **Family Felidae**

Identifying Features
This is a large, unspotted, leopard-sized cat that has short yellowish-brown fur. Its long tail has a dark brown tip.

Measurements
Total length, 90 inches (2.3 m); tail, 31 inches (790 mm); hind foot, 12 inches (300 mm); ear, 4 inches (100 mm); weight, 160 pounds (70 kg). Females are about 10% smaller than the males.

Habitat
Mountain lions formerly occurred throughout most of this region. Still present in all but the most human-modified areas, they are most common in rural situations.

Life Habits
Mountain lions are active throughout the year, mostly at night. Their usual food consists of deer, rabbits, and rodents. When they are hungry and domestic animals are available, they may kill sheep, goats, calves, pigs, cows, and even horses. A large area is needed to provide a continuing food source year after year. Feeding areas often include as much as 25 miles around the den. Populations of large cats were never high, despite various old-timer tales. At present, in some areas, populations are as dense as 10 animals per 100 square miles. Probably this has always been normal in good habitats. Females have dens in caves or cliffs where two to five kittens are born in the spring.

144

Mountain lion

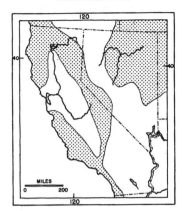

Bobcat

Felis rufus

Order Carnivora   **Family Felidae**

Identifying Features

This is a short-tailed cat with tufted ears, large paws, and a large, broad head. It is larger than the house cat. The color is a reddish brown with black spots.

Measurements

Total length, 37 inches (940 mm); tail, 6 inches (150 mm); hind foot, 7.5 inches (190 mm); ear, 3.2 inches (80 mm); weight, 24 pounds (10.9 kg).

Habitat

Bobcats occur throughout most of this area, being most common in brush and forest-edge situations or in rocky canyons. They even occur in city suburbs.

Life Habits

Bobcats are active throughout the year, mostly at night. Food is mainly small rodents and rabbits. Squirrels, porcupines, birds, and carrion are also eaten. Rarely, lambs and small goats are killed and eaten. Most of their hunting is done within two miles of their den. Dens are in rock crevices or in holes under rocks, fallen trees, or tree stumps. Some dens are in hollow trees. After a gestation period of 50 to 60 days, a litter of one to four (usually two) blind, helpless young are born. Although most young are born in April or May, some have been born in every month of the year. *See related species 95.*

Bobcat

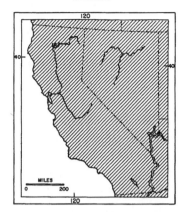

Wild pig

Sus scrofa

Order Artiodactyla   **Family Suidae**

Identifying Features

This heavy-bodied, short-legged mammal is typically pig-shaped. It has four toes on each foot, but most of the weight is borne on the central two. The upper tusks curve outward and upward. The skin is thinly covered with coarse hair, the ears are hairy, the snout is naked. The tail is short, small in diameter, and not tufted.

Measurements

Total length, 51 inches (1.3 m); tail, 12 inches (300 mm); ear, 6 inches (150 mm); weight, 300 pounds (130 kg). Some old males reach weights in excess of 600 pounds (260 kg).

Habitat

Wild pigs are natives of the Old World. In California, they live in dense forests and in adjacent bushy areas.

Life Habits

Most are descendants of escaped domestic swine. Some are descendants of introduced Old World Wild pigs (the same species). They are most active in early morning or late afternoon. Family groups consisting of a sow and her young are common. Herds of up to 50 have been seen. Boars are solitary. Food includes grasses, fungi, roots, bulbs, fruits, nuts, berries, frogs, birds, snakes, and dead animals. At birth, the piglets are brown with nine or ten longitudinal black stripes.

Wild pig

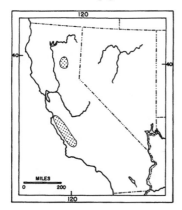

Wapiti or Elk

Cervus elaphus

Order Artiodactyla   **Family Cervidae**

Identifying Features

This is a large deer that has a patch of pale yellowish hair on the rump around the small, white tail. The color is a reddish brown. Males have a mane on the neck and, in late summer and fall, large antlers. The antlers of older males generally have six branches, the lowest of which (the brow tine, nearest the head) is well-developed.

Measurements

Total length, 98 inches (2.5 m); tail, 6 inches (150 mm); hind foot, 22 inches (550 mm); ear, 8 inches (200 mm); weight, usually about 600 pounds, but over 1000 pounds (260-450 kg) has been recorded. Females are about 10% smaller than males.

Habitat

Elk once occurred in the grasslands of central and northern California and the mountain meadows of eastern Nevada. Those in the coastal rain forests were called Roosevelt elk; in the central valley and foothills, Tule elk. Populations today have been reduced to a few scattered herds.

Life Habits

Elk formerly lived in herds of ten to several hundred. These herds migrated from high mountain meadows in the summer to lowlands in the winter. Food is a variety of grasses, sedges, and fresh growth on bushes and trees. A single calf, born in May or June, weighs about 30 pounds (13.5 kg) and is brownish with light spots.

Wapiti or Elk

(vertical lines = former range,
dots = introduced,
diagonal lines = residual
populations)

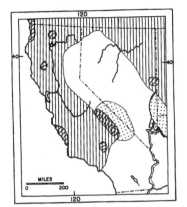

sandy Truett

Mule deer

Odocoileus hemionus

Order Artiodactyla   **Family Cervidae**

Identifying Features

This deer is smaller than the Elk. Its tail is narrow and mostly white, but with at least a black tip, if not black on the whole top surface. Color is a reddish brown in the summer, grayish in the winter. Males have antlers from late summer until January. The main forks of the antlers are equally branched.

Measurements

Total length, 63 inches (1.6 m); tail, 8 inches (200 mm); hind foot, 18 inches (450 mm); ear, 8 inches (200 mm); weight, to 350 pounds (150 kg).

Habitat

Mule deer occur from coniferous forests down to shrubby grasslands and desert areas. They are found most often in broken country, generally in brush or at a forest edge.

Life Habits

Mule deer are active mainly in the early morning and late evening, or on moonlit nights. They move to higher mountain elevations during the spring and summer. In the fall and winter, they often live in small herds. They feed mostly on shrubs and twigs, but also eat some grasses and herbs. After a gestation period of about 210 days, one or two young are born. They are furred at birth, have their eyes open, and can follow their mother within minutes. *See related species 96.*

Mule deer

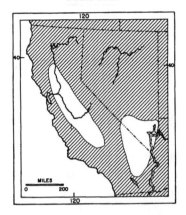

Pronghorn

Antilocapra americana

Order Artiodactyla   **Family Bovidae**

Identifying Features

The Pronghorn is a hoofed mammal that is slightly smaller than the Mule deer. It has black horns—not antlers—both in females and males. Unlike the horns of the Bison and sheep, the outer portion (horn sheath) is shed each year. The color is brownish. A large, white rump patch, and two white bands across the throat are characteristic.

Measurements

Total length, 51 inches (1.3 m); tail, 6 inches (150 mm); hind foot, 17 inches (430 mm); weight, to 125 pounds (57 kg).

Habitat

Pronghorns are residents of bushy grasslands and sagebrush flats of northeastern California and northwestern Nevada.

Life Habits

Pronghorns are active during most parts of the day. They feed on a wide variety of brush and forbs as well as some grasses. Sagebrush and rabbit brush are favorites. In much of their range, they move down slopes to valleys to spend the winter months. They move in herds, with groups of ten to 60 being common. For short distances, Pronghorns can run at 55 miles (88 km) per hour. After a gestation period of about eight months, one or two young are born, usually in June. They can follow their mother within minutes of birth. In captivity, Pronghorns can live up to 15 years.

154

Pronghorn
(lines = former range, dots = present range)

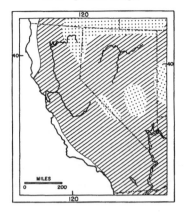

Bison

Bison bison

Order Artiodactyla   **Family Bovidae**

Identifying Features
The Bison, also called American buffalo, is almost cowlike in appearance, but is generally larger and chunkier. Its horns (in both males and females) are bent outward and upward. The forehead and neck are short, the face is broad, and the shoulders have a large hump. The tail is short and tufted. Hair on the shoulders, head, and neck is long and the chin is bearded. The color is dark brownish.

Measurements
Total length, 11 feet (3.4 m); tail, 25 inches (625 mm); hind foot, 24 inches (600 mm); weight, to 1800 pounds (820 kg). Females are generally about one-third smaller than males.

Habitat
Bison once occurred in the grasslands of northeastern California. They were probably eliminated from the region more than a century ago. They were introduced on Santa Catalina Island (off Los Angeles) in the 1930s.

Life Habits
In the past, Bison occurred in herds that seasonally moved north and south in the Great Plains to take advantage of available food. In parts of the range, this led to temporary local concentrations that led some hunters and writers to think that Bison populations were limitless. Some recent guesses place the original population at about 60 million. By 1890, the total was less than 1000.

Bison

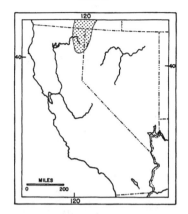

Helen Wilson

Mountain sheep

Ovis canadensis

Order Artiodactyla   **Family Bovidae**

Identifying Features
The Mountain sheep is a large sheep that has large, heavy-curving horns in males (more slender and less curved in females). It is brownish to grayish in color and has a large white rump patch.

Measurements
Total length, 70 inches (1.8 m); tail, 5.1 inches (130 mm); hind foot, 16.5 inches (420 mm); weight, to 300 pounds (130 kg). Females are 15% smaller.

Habitat
Mountain sheep, also known as Bighorn sheep, once lived in most of the foothills and mountains. In competition with man and domestic animals, they have been eliminated from much of the area.

Life Habits
Most feeding by Mountain sheep occurs in the early morning, but they may be active any time of the day. Food is a mixture of grasses, branches of woody plants, and various herbs. They generally occur in small bands. Some large bands include 12 to 15, or even more, individuals. Their need for drinking water restricts their occurrence in desert regions. After a gestation period of about six months, a single lamb is born in March or April.

Mountain sheep

**(lines = former range,
dots = introduced)**

Sandy Truett

Related Species

The following mammals could all have been listed in the preceding pages. However, most are not only close relatives to the ones discussed above but also much like their "relative" in size and appearance. In some cases, the "major species" listed above does not occur throughout the region, but is often replaced by one of these "related species." Obviously, in such places, the "related species" should be given a "major" status.

1. **Mount Lyell shrew** (*Sorex lyelli*). This species is similar in size to the Vagrant shrew. It is brownish above, gray below, and has a markedly bicolored tail. Distribution is restricted to higher elevations of Mount Lyell and adjacent areas of Mono and Tuolumne counties, California. Much of the higher elevation of Yosemite National Park is included in this range. Map 1, area 1.

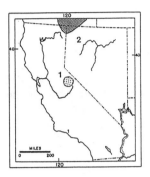

Map 1

2. **Preble's shrew** (*Sorex preblei*). This shrew is closely related to the Mount Lyell shrew; similar in color and slightly smaller in size. It occurs at elevations above 4200 feet (1300 m) in northeastern California and adjacent Nevada. Map 1, area 2.

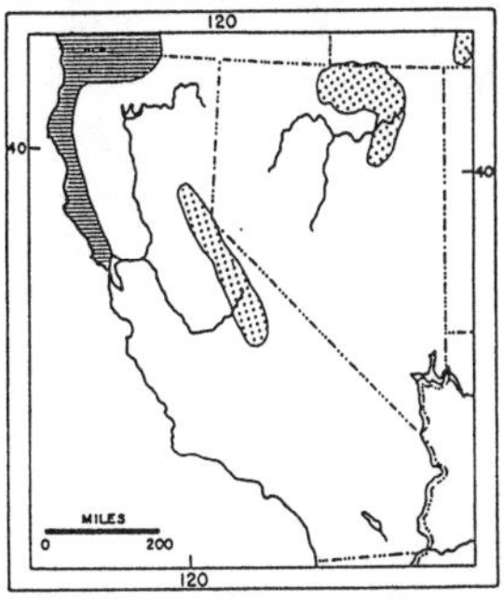

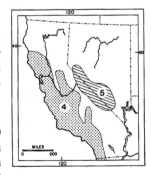

Map 2

3. **Montane shrew** (*Sorex monticolus*) and **Fog shrew** (*Sorex sonomae*) are closely related. Both are similar to the Vagrant shrew and, until recently, were considered the same species. Map 2: lines = Fog shrew, dots = Montane shrew.

4. **Ornate shrew** (*Sorex ornatus*). This species is slightly smaller than the Vagrant shrew. It is lighter in color, being grayish brown above, lighter below, and having an indistinctly bicolored tail. It occurs from sea level to elevations of 7500 feet (2500 m). Map 3, area 4.

5. **Inyo shrew** (*Sorex tenellus*). This species is closely related to the Ornate shrew. It is similar in size and is slightly paler in color. It occurs at elevations of from 5500 to 9500 feet (1800-3100 m). Map 3, area 5.

6. **Northern water shrew** (*Sorex palustris*). This is a large shrew: length, 6 inches (150 mm); tail, 3 inches (77 mm); hind foot, 0.8 inch (20 mm); weight, 0.5 ounce (14 g). It lives in and near mountain streams. The body is black

Map 3

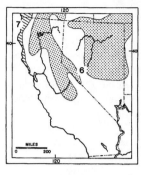

Map 4

to gray above, lighter below. The tail is bicolored, dark above. The hind feet have a fringe of stiff hairs that help trap air bubbles, permitting this shrew to walk on the surface of the water for short distances. Map 4, area 6.

7. **Pacific marsh shrew** (*Sorex bendirii*). This species is the largest North American shrew, reaching a weight of 0.6 ounce (16 g). It is dark brown above and below, often has white tipped hairs, and has a tail that is the same color above and below. It occurs in marshes and other wet situations in the coastal forests of northern California. Map 4, area 7.

8. **Trowbridge's shrew** (*Sorex trowbridgii*). This species is about the size of the Vagrant shrew. The back is gray to black, the belly is paler, and the tail is bicolored. It occurs in coniferous forests in much of northern California. Map 5, area 8.

9. **Merriam's shrew** (*Sorex merriami*). This shrew is smaller than the Vagrant shrew. It usually lives in drier places than most other shrews—open sagebrush, grasslands, dry woodlands. It is light-colored, gray above and white below. The tail is white. Measurements are: total length, 3.8 inches (95 mm); tail, 1.5 inches (38 mm); hind foot, 0.5 inch (12 mm); weight, 0.2 ounce (5 g). Map 5, area 9.

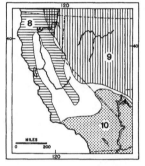

Map 5

10. **Desert shrew** (*Notiosorex crawfordi*). This is a small shrew that has larger ears than other shrews. It occurs in semiarid situations. Measurements are: total length, 3.5 inches (90 mm); tail, 1.4 inches (35 mm); hind foot, 0.5 inch (12 mm); weight, 0.2 ounces (5 g). Map 5, area 10.

11. **Shrew-mole** (*Neurotrichus gibbsii*). This is the smallest mole in North America. The tail is long and hairy. The forelegs are little modified for

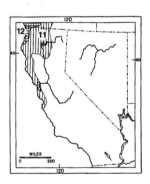

Map 6

digging. Measurements are: total length, 4.7 inches (120 mm); tail, 1.5 inches (38 mm); hind foot, 0.6 inch (15 mm); weight, 0.3 ounce (9 g). Map 6, area 11.

12. **Townsend's mole** (*Scapanus townsendi*). This species has the shape of the typical mole. Its color is almost black. It occurs in meadows, fields, and openings in the coastal coniferous forests of northwestern California. Measurements are: total length, 9 inches (220 mm); tail, 1.6 inches (40 mm); hind foot, 1 inch (25 mm); weight, 4.3 ounces (120 g). Map 6, area 12.

13. **Coast mole** (*Scapanus orarius*). This species occurs in deciduous forests in coastal northern California. It is intermediate in size between the preceding species and the Broad-footed mole. Measurements are: total length, 6.2 inches (160 mm); tail, 1.4 inches (35 mm); hind foot, 0.8 inch (20 mm). It is black in color and its tail is almost naked. No map,

14. **Yuma myotis** (*Myotis yumanensis*). This bat is about the same size as the Little brown bat. It feeds almost exclusively on insects that are captured as they fly over permanent streams and ponds. Map 7.

Map 7

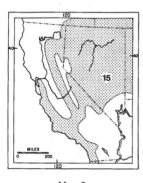

Map 8

15. **Western small-footed myotis** (*Myotis ciliolabrum*). This bat has a shorter forearm (about 1.5 inches–37 mm) and weighs less (0.2 ounce–6 g) than the Little brown bat. Day roosts are often in tiny rock crevices, usually in forested areas. Map 8.

16. **Cave myotis** (*Myotis velifer*). A larger bat than the Little brown bat, its summer roosts are in mines and caves along the lower Colorado River. Its winter hibernal are in the mountains of Arizona. Measurements are: total length, 3.8 inches (95 mm); tail, 1.6 inches (40 mm); hind foot, 0.4 inch (10 mm); ear, 0.6 inch (15 mm); forearm, 1.6 inches (42 mm); weight, 0.4 ounce (12 g). Map 9, area 16.

17. **Long-legged myotis** (*Myotis volans*). This species lives in forests, usually at higher elevations. Its wings are furred on the lower surface to the elbow; the interfemoral membrane is furred to about the knee. It is similar in size to the Little brown bat but has shorter ears and is lighter in weight, 0.3 ounce (9 g). Map 9, area 17.

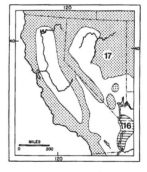

Map 9

18. **Fringed myotis** (*Myotis thysanodes*). This bat has longer ears, 0.7 inch (18 mm) and forearms, 1.7 inches (43 mm) than the Little brown bat. It has a well-developed fringe of stiff hairs extending from the edge of the interfemoral membrane. Map 10.

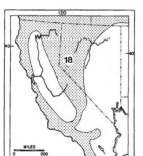

Map 10

163

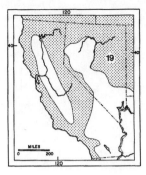

Map 11

19. **Long-eared myotis** (*Myotis evotis*). This bat has longer ears, 0.9 inch (22 mm), longer forearms, 1.6 inches (40 mm), and lighter weight, 0.25 ounce (7 g) than the Little brown bat. Its ears, black in color, are longer than any myotis in the area. Coniferous forests are its usual habitat. Map 11.

20. **California myotis** (*Myotis californicus*). This is a small-footed myotis (0.24 inch–6 mm) that is light in color and has contrasting black ears, wing membranes, and interfemoral membrane. It is most common in open grasslands and deserts. Map 12.

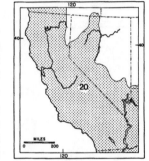

Map 12

21. **Allen's big-eared bat** (*Idionycteris phyllotis*). This rarely seen bat is larger and has longer ears than Townsend's big-eared bat. It weighs about 0.5 ounce (14 g) and has ears that are about 1.6 inches (40 mm) in length. Map 13.

22. **Pocketed free-tailed bat** (*Nyctinomops femorosaccus*). This species is larger than the Brazilian free-tailed bat. Its ears are joined at their bases. Measurements are: total length, 4 inches (100 mm); tail, 1.5 inches (38 mm); hind foot, 0.4 inch (10 mm); weight, 0.55 ounce (16 g); forearm, 1.9 inches (47 mm). Map 14, area 22.

23. **Big free-tailed bat** (*Nyctinomops macrotis*). This large relative of the Brazilian free-tailed bat has a forearm that is 2.4 inches (60 mm) in length and weighs 0.9 ounce (25 g). Its ears are broadly joined at the midline. Day roosts are generally in high rock crevices. Map 14, area 23.

24. **Brush rabbit** (*Sylvilagus bachmani*). This rabbit has short ears, a short tail, and small hind legs. Measurements are: total length, 12.8 inches (325 mm); tail, 1.6 inches (40 mm); hind foot, 3 inches (77 mm); ear, 2.3 inches (60 mm); weight, 1.7 pounds (750 g). It lives at the edge of dense chaparral or other heavy-brush areas. Map 15, area 24.

Map 13

25. **Pygmy rabbit** (*Sylvilagus idahoensis*). This is the smallest rabbit in North America. Measurements are: total length, 10.8 inches (275 mm); tail, 1 inch (25 mm); hind foot 2.6 inches (65 mm), ear, 1.8 inches (45 mm);

Map 14

Map 15

weight, 14 ounces (400 g). It has a whitish spot on each side of the nose and a tail that is gray, both above and below. It generally occurs in sagebrush. Map 15, area 25.

26. Desert cottontail (*Sylvilagus audubonii*). This cottontail is slightly smaller (weight, 2 pounds–900 g) and lighter in color than Nuttall's cottontail. It usually lives in desert grasslands, creosote, and desert areas below 4000 feet (1300 m). Map 16.

27. Black-tailed jack rabbit (*Lepus californicus*). This jack rabbit is usually found at lower elevations (below 6000 feet–1830 m) than the white-tailed jack rabbit. It occurs in grasslands, barren areas, and deserts. A distinct black stripe is on the top of the tail. The two species are similar in size. Map 17.

28. Lodgepole chipmunk (*Tamias speciosus*). This chipmunk has a unique brown color on the top side of the head. It is restricted in distribution to areas of red fir and lodgepole pine that have a mixture of manzanita present. Map 18, area 28.

29. Sonoma chipmunk (*Tamias sonomae*). This chipmunk is larger (total length, 12 inches–

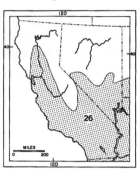

Map 16

300 mm) and darker in color than other chipmunks species. It occurs at low elevations (below 6000 feet–1830 m) in northwestern California. Bushy and open areas in pine forests (redwood and yellow pine) are favored habitats. Map 18, area 29.

30. Yellow-pine chipmunk (*Tamias amoenus*). This brightly colored species lives in open forests of northern California and northwestern Nevada. It is active throughout most of the year. Short periods of hibernation occur during the most severe winter storms. Map 19, area 30.

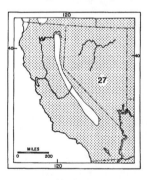

Map 17

31. Merriam's chipmunk (*Tamias merriami*). This species has a very curious distribution (see map). They live at the upper edge of the chaparral upward to about the lower piñon-juniper forest areas (7000 feet–2200 m) in southern California. Map 19, area 31.

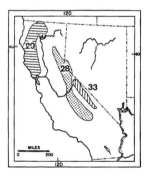

Map 18

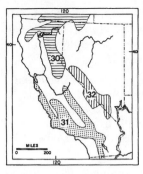

Map 19

32. **Panamint chipmunk** (*Tamias panamintinus*). This chipmunk is found only in rocky areas of piñon-juniper forests in southwest Nevada and adjacent California. Map 19, area 32.

33. **Alpine chipmunk** (*Tamias alpinus*). This species is found only at high elevations (above 8000 feet–2600 m) in the Sierra Nevada Mountains of east-central California. There they inhabit rocky areas, especially rock slides and talus slopes. Map 18, area 33.

34. **Yellow-cheeked chipmunk** (*Tamias ochrogenys*). This is another chipmunk with a limited distribution. It occurs only in redwood forests of coastal northern California. It and the next two species are extremely closely related and similar in size and color. Map 20, area 34.

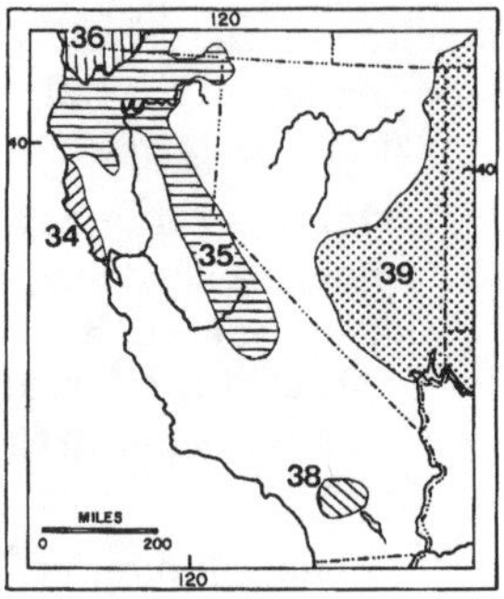

35. **Allen's chipmunk** (*Tamias senex*). See species 34 above. This chipmunk occurs in forests of northern California. Map 20, area 35.

36. **Siskiyou chipmunk** (*Tamias siskiyou*). See species 34 and 35 above. This chipmunk occurs in part of northern California and adjacent Oregon. Map 20, area 36.

37. **Uinta chipmunk** (*Tamias umbrinus*). This chipmunk differs only in minor details from several other species. It occurs in mountain regions of much of northeastern Nevada and a small area of California. It spends much of the winter in hibernation. Map 21, area 37.

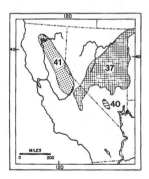

Map 20

38. **California chipmunk** (*Tamias obscurus*). This is a pale relative of Merriam's chipmunk. It occurs only in two very small areas in southern California (Joshua Tree National Monument and the San Bernardino National Forest). Two other small populations occur in Baja California. Map 20, area 38.

39. **Cliff chipmunk** (*Tamias dorsalis*). This is a grayish chipmunk with indistinct stripes on its body. It is often seen at lower mountain elevations and is more restricted to rocky areas than most other chipmunks. Map 20, area 39.

40. **Palmer's chipmunk** (*Tamias palmeri*). This species, perhaps a close relative of the Uinta chipmunk, is known only from the isolated Spring Mountain area of southern Nevada. Map 21, area 40.

Map 21

166

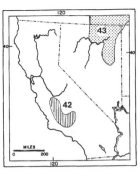

Map 22

41. **Long-eared chipmunk** (*Tamias quadrimaculatus*). This species is restricted to pine and fir forests of the Sierra Nevadas from 3600 to 7300 feet (1100-2300 m) in east-central California. It has a large white spot just below each ear. Map 21, area 39.

42. **Nelson's antelope squirrel** (*Ammospermophilus nelsoni*). This species is also called the San Joaquin antelope squirrel. Larger and more buff than the White-tailed antelope squirrel, this species occurs only in Kern, King, and western Fresno counties, California. It is listed by California as a rare mammal. Map 22, area 42.

43. **Richardson's ground squirrel** (*Spermophilus richardsoni*). This species is larger than Townsend's ground squirrel: total length, 12 inches (300 mm); tail, 3 inches (75 mm); hind foot, 1.8 inches (45 mm); weight, 14 ounces (400 g). It is somewhat solitary, but often several congregate in patches of good habitat—usually open areas of short vegetation. Map 22, area 43.

44. **Belding's ground squirrel** (*Spermophilus beldingi*). This species has a much larger hind foot than Townsend's ground squirrel. Measurements are: total length, 10.8 inches (275 mm); tail, 2.5 inches (65 mm); hind foot, 1.8 inches (45 mm); weight, 11 ounces (300 g). It is sometimes a pest in hay and alfalfa fields. Map 23, area 44.

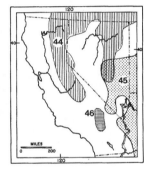

Map 23

45. **Rock squirrel** (*Spermophilus variegatus*). This species occurs in rocky situations from high mountains to the desert floor. It is about the same size as the California ground squirrel. Its color is generally paler, a mottled grayish brown. Map 23, area 45.

46. **Mohave ground squirrel** (*Spermophilus mohavensis*). This species is known only from a few localities in the Mohave Desert. It is listed by California as a rare mammal. Map 23, area 46.

47. **Fox squirrel** (*Sciurus niger*). This species, a native of the eastern United States, has been introduced into various city parks. The large bushy tail with buff-tipped hairs is distinctive. It is the largest North American tree squirrel. Measurements are: total length, 23.6 inches (600 mm); tail, 10.8 inches (275 mm); hind foot, 3 inches (75 mm); weight, 1.8 pounds (800 g). No map.

48. **Gray squirrel** (*Sciurus carolinensis*). This is a native of the eastern United States that has been successfully introduced into a few parks in this region. Measurements are: total length, 19 inches (480 mm); tail, 9 inches (225 mm); hind foot, 2.6 inches (65 mm); weight, 2 pounds (900 g). The tail bush appears to be flattened and has long gray hairs that are tipped with white, giving a silvery appearance. No map.

167

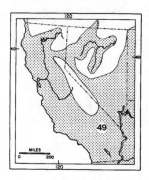

Map 24

49. **Botta's pocket gopher** (*Thomomys bottae*). In general, a given area has only a single kind of pocket gopher. Even when two species do occur in the same general region, they occupy different habitats. This species inhabits valleys and low elevations when they occur near another species of pocket gopher. Map 24.

50. **Western pocket gopher** (*Thomomys mazama*). This species resembles the others in the region. Map 25, area 50.

51. **Mountain pocket gopher** (*Thomomys monticola*). This species resembles the other gophers in the region. Map 25, area 51.

52. **Great Basin pocket mouse** (*Perognathus parvus*). Measurements of this silky pocket mouse are: total length, 6.9 inches (175 mm); tail, 3.3 inches (85 mm); hind foot, 1 inch (25 mm); weight, 0.8 ounce (22 g). Map 26, area 52.

53. **White-eared pocket mouse** (*Perognathus alticola*). This species is closely related to the Great Basin pocket mouse. It is similar in size but lighter in color. It occurs only in a very small part of California. Map 26, area 53.

Map 25

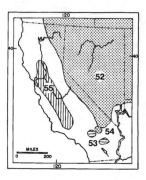

Map 26

54. **Yellow-eared pocket mouse** (*Perognathus xanthonotus*). This is closely related to the White-eared pocket mouse. Map 26, area 54.

55. **San Joaquin pocket mouse** (*Perognathus inornatus*). This medium-sized silky pocket mouse is restricted to areas of weed or grass-covered fine soils. Measurements are: total length, 5.7 inches (145 mm); tail, 2.8 inches (72 mm); hind foot, 0.8 inch (20 mm); weight, 0.5 ounce (14 g). Map 26, area 55.

56. **Long-tailed pocket mouse** (*Perognathus formosus*). The pelage of this large species is harsher than that of most silky pocket mice. Measurements are: total length, 8 inches (200 mm); tail, 4 inches (100 mm); hind foot, 1 inch (25 mm); weight, 0.8 ounce (22 g). Map 27.

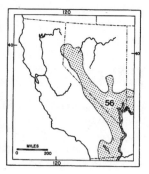

Map 27

57. **Bailey's pocket mouse** (*Chaetodipus baileyi*). This the largest pocket mouse in the area. It occurs on rocky slopes in the desert of southern California. Measurements are: total length, 7.9 inches (200 mm); tail, 4.4 inches (110 mm); hind foot, 1 inch (25 mm); ear, 0.4 inch (9 mm); weight, 1 ounce (28 g). Map 28, area 57.

58. **Desert pocket mouse** (*Chaetodipus penicillatus*). This relative of the Spiny pocket mouse occurs along dry streambeds or washes in the deserts of southern California. Its total length is about 6 inches (150 mm); weight, 0.7 ounce (19 g). Map 29, area 58.

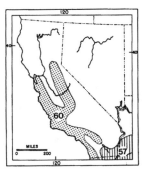

Map 28

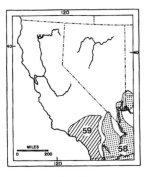

Map 29

59. **San Diego pocket mouse** (*Chaetodipus fallax*). This rough-haired pocket mouse has scattered spines on the rump and some stiff white hairs on the hips. About the size of the Desert pocket mouse, it is restricted to bushy slopes in southern California and adjacent Mexico. Map 29, area 59.

60. **California pocket mouse** (*Chaetodipus californicus*). This rough-haired pocket mouse is brownish gray in color and has scattered, stiff white hairs on the rump. It occurs on the coast and some interior valleys in southern California. Map 28, area 60.

61. **Merriam's kangaroo rat** (*Dipodomys merriami*). This species occurs in a wide variety of habitats, mostly in creosote and sagebrush areas of the deserts. Measurements are: total length, 9.5 inches (240 mm); tail, 5.5 inches (140 mm); hind foot, 1.5 inches (38 mm); ear. 0.5 inch (14 mm); weight, 1.5 ounces (42 g). Map 30, area 61.

62. **Chisel-toothed kangaroo rat** (*Dipodomys microps*). This species occurs in sagebrush and piñon-juniper woodlands. It is larger than the Ord's kangaroo rat. Measurements are: total length, 11 inches (280 mm); tail, 6.7 inches (170 mm); hind foot, 1.7 inches (42 mm); weight, 2.1 ounces (60 g). Map 31, area 62.

63. **Stephen's kangaroo rat** (*Dipodomys stephensii*). This species measures: total length, 11.4 inches (290 mm); tail, 6.7 inches (170 mm); hind foot, 1.7 inches (42 mm); weight, 3 ounces (84 g). This large species is known only from the San Jacinto valley of southern California. It is on the California list of rare mammals. Map 31, area 63.

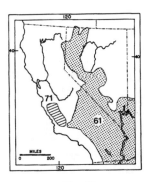

Map 30

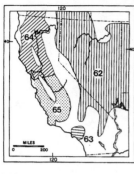

Map 31

64. **California kangaroo rat** (*Dipodomys californicus*). This species is externally almost identical to the next species but differs in the structure of its chromosomes. Map 31, area 64.

65. **Heermann's kangaroo rat** (*Dipodomys heermanni*). This species lives in open, sloping grasslands and in meadows in live-oak and pine woodlands. Measurements are: total length, 11.8 inches (300 mm); tail, 7.5 inches (190 mm); hind foot, 1.6 inches (42 mm); weight, 2.5 ounces (70 g). Populations in the Morro Bay area are listed by the United States Fish and Wildlife Service as an endangered species. Map 31, area 65.

66. **Giant kangaroo rat** (*Dipodomys ingens*). This is the largest of the kangaroo rats. It occurs in open grasslands in the San Joaquin valley. Measurements are: total length, 13 inches (330 mm); tail, 7.5 inches (190 mm); hind foot, 2 inches (49 mm); weight, 5.5 ounces (155 g). Map 32, area 66.

67. **Panamint kangaroo rat** (*Dipodomys panamintinus*). This species occurs in piñon-juniper areas and in creosote shrub areas at slightly lower elevations. Measurements are: total length, 12.6 inches (320 mm); tail, 7 inches (175 mm); hind foot, 1.8 inches (46 mm); weight, 3 ounces (85 g). Map 32, area 67.

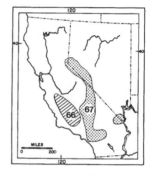

Map 32

68. **Narrow-faced kangaroo rat** (*Dipodomys venustus*). This close relative of Heermann's kangaroo rat occurs only in parts of Monterey and Santa Cruz counties, California. Measurements are: total length, 12.2 inches (310 mm); tail, 7.5 inches (190 mm); hind foot, 1.8 inches (45 mm); weight, 3.9 ounces (110 g). Map 33, area 68.

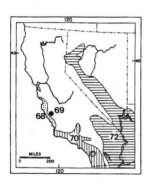

Map 33

69. **Big-eared kangaroo rat** (*Dipodomys elephantinus*). This species, like the preceding one, is also closely related to Heermann's kangaroo rat. It is known only from part of San Benito County, California. Map 33, area 69.

70. **Agile kangaroo rat** (*Dipodomys agilis*). Like the two preceding species, this one is also a close relative of Heermann's kangaroo rat. It occurs in brush-covered areas of sand and gravel in southwestern California. Measurements are: total length, 11.8 inches (300 mm); tail, 7.1 inches (180 mm); hind foot, 1.7 inches (43 mm); weight, 2.5 ounces (70 g). Map 33, area 70.

170

71. **Fresno kangaroo rat** (*Dipodomys nitratoides*). This species is almost identical in size with Merriam's kangaroo rat and is considered by some to be the same species. Populations near Fresno are listed by California as an endangered species. Map 30, area 71.

72. **Desert kangaroo rat** (*Dipodomys deserti*). This is a large species that lives in areas of loose, sandy desert soil. Measurements include: length, 13 inches (325 mm) and weight, 3.5 ounces (100 g). Map 33, area 72.

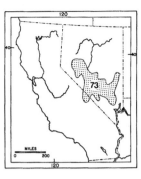

Map 34

73. **Pale kangaroo mouse** (*Microdipodops pallidus*). This species differs from the Dark kangaroo mouse in having a paler color. The top of the tail lacks the black tip, being about the same color as the back. Areas of fine sand in the desert are its usual habitat. Map 34.

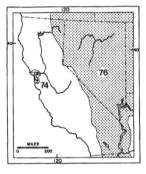

Map 35

74. **Salt-marsh harvest mouse** (*Reithrodontomys raviventris*). This species differs only slightly from the Western harvest mouse. It has a buff, not white, belly. It occurs only in various salt marshes around San Francisco Bay. These habitats are being greatly modified by man. As a result, these mice are being reduced in numbers and are currently listed on the California and the United States Fish and Wildlife Service lists of endangered species. Map 35, area 74.

75. **Cactus mouse** (*Peromyscus eremicus*). This species occurs in the sandy soils of low deserts. Measurements are: total length, 7.5 inches (190 mm); tail, 3.9 inches (100 mm); hind foot, 0.8 inch (20 mm); ear, 0.8 inch (20 mm); weight, 0.7 ounce (21 g). Map 36, area 75.

76. **Canyon mouse** (*Peromyscus crinitus*). This species differs from the Deer mouse in having longer, softer fur and a tufted tail that is more than half of the total length. It occurs on rocky slopes and canyon walls in situations not normally occupied by other mice of the genus *Peromyscus*. Map 35, area 76.

77. **California mouse** (*Peromyscus californicus*). This is the largest member of this genus. It occurs only in areas of dense chaparral (brush vegetation). Measurements are: total length, 10.2 inches (260 mm); tail, 5.7 inches (145 mm); hind foot, 1.1 inches (27 mm); ear, 0.9 inch (23 mm); weight, 1.4 ounces (40 g). Map 36, area 77.

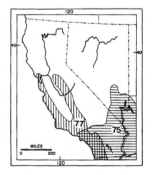

Map 36

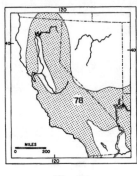

Map 37

78. **Brush mouse** (*Peromyscus boylii*). This species lives in rocky areas in brush and forests. Its tail is tufted and is slightly longer than the head and body. Measurements include: total length, 7.5 inches (190 mm); tail, 4 inches (100 mm); hind foot, 0.8 inch (20 mm); ear, 0.8 inch (20 mm); weight, 0.9 ounce (25 g). Map 37.

79. **Piñon mouse** (*Peromyscus truei*). This long-eared mouse occurs in rocky areas of piñon-juniper in most nondesert habitats of this region. Measurements are: total length, 8.3 inches (210 mm); tail, 4 inches (100 mm); hind foot, 1 inch (25 mm); ear, 1 inch (25 mm); weight, 1 ounce (28 g). Map 38.

80. **Southern grasshopper mouse** (*Onychomys torridus*). This species is slightly smaller and longer-tailed than the Northern grasshopper mouse. In areas of central Nevada and southern California, where both occur, this species inhabits the drier habitats with sparser vegetation. Map 39.

81. **Arizona cotton rat** (*Sigmodon arizonae*). This cotton rat is known in this region only from a few records from southern Nevada and adjacent California. Externally it differs from the Hispid cotton rat in a few minor nonobvious features. In the structure of its chromosomes, the differences are markedly distinct. Map 40.

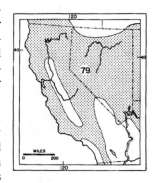

Map 38

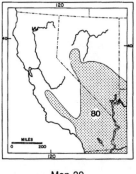

Map 39

82. **Dusky-footed woodrat** (*Neotoma fuscipes*). This rat-tailed species is about the same size as the White-throated woodrat. It occurs in the deserts and piñon-juniper areas of Nevada and most of southern California. Map 41, area 82.

83. **White-throated woodrat** (*Neotoma albigula*). This rat-tailed woodrat occurs on dry plains at lower elevations in a few localities in southern Nevada and eastern California. Map 41, area 83.

84. **Desert woodrat** (*Neotoma lepida*). This rat-tailed woodrat lives in desert and piñon-juniper areas in part of California. Map 42.

85. **White-footed vole** (*Arborimus albipes*). This vole is larger and has a longer tail than the heather vole. The tops of the feet are usually white. Measurements are: total length, 6.7 inches (170 mm); tail, 2.6 inches (65 mm); hind foot, 0.4 inch (10 mm). Map 43, area 85.

172

86. **Red tree vole** (*Arborimus longicaudus*). This species is similar in size and lives in much the same area as the White-footed vole. However, it lives in trees and rarely descends to the ground. It builds a nest in a tree and feeds on the needles of Douglas firs and a few other conifers. Map 43, area 86.

87. **Montane vole** (*Microtus montanus*). This short-tailed (1.7 inches–42 mm) vole lives in burrows around the bases of grasses, especially in mountain meadows from 4000 to over 10,000 feet (1220-3300 m). Map 43, area 87.

Map 40

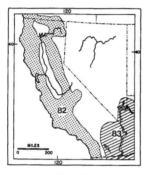

Map 41

88. **Townsend's vole** (*Microtus townsendii*). The largest vole in the region, it lives in wet lowlands in northwestern California. Measurements are: total length, 8.9 inches (225 mm); tail, 2.6 inches (65 mm); hind foot, 1 inch (25 mm); ear, 0.6 inch (15 mm); weight, 2.8 ounces (80 g). Map 44, area 88.

89. **California vole** (*Microtus californicus*). This species lives in dry upland meadows in much of California. Measurements are: total length, 6.7 inches (170 mm); tail, 1.6 inches (40 mm); hind foot, 0.8 inch (21 mm); ear, 0.6 inch (15 mm); weight, 2.1 ounces (60 g). Populations along the Amargosa River in Inyo County, California, sometimes called the Amargosa vole (*Microtus californicus scirpensis*), are listed by California as a rare mammal. Map 44, area 89.

90. **Creeping vole** (*Microtus oregoni*). This vole lives along the Pacific coast of northwestern California from sea level to 6000 feet (1830 m) elevation. Measurements are: total length, 5.5 inches (140 mm); tail, 1.7 inches (42 mm); hind foot, 0.7 inch (17 mm) ear, 0.4 inch (10 mm); weight, 0.9 ounce (25 g). Map 45.

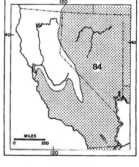

Map 42

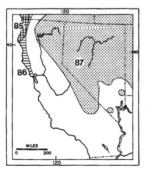

Map 43

91. **Black rat** (*Rattus rattus*). This is also an introduced species from the Old World. It has a longer tail and longer ears than the Norway rat. It is found most commonly in large cities, especially around seaports. No map.

173

Map 44

92. **Pacific jumping mouse** (*Zapus trinotatus*). This species occurs in northwestern California and adjacent Oregon. Map 46.

93. **Channel Islands gray fox** (*Urocyon littoralis*). This small fox is restricted to the islands of Santa Catalina, San Nicolas, San Miguel, Santa Cruz, and Santa Rosa, off the coast of southern California. Its total length is less than 31 inches (800 mm); its tail is less than 12 inches (300 mm). It is listed by California as a rare mammal. No map.

94. **Fisher** (*Martes pennanti*). A Fisher is larger than a Marten. Males weigh up to 15 pounds (7 kg). At present, they have similar ranges. No map.

95. **Lynx** (*Lynx canadensis*). This cat has a shorter tail than the Bobcat (4 inches–100 mm in the Lynx; 5 inches–125 mm in the Bobcat). Its tail is black-tipped, both above and below while the Bobcat's tail is black only on the top side. Lynx generally occur in forests above 7000 feet (2130 m). No map.

96. **White-tailed deer** (*Odocoileus virginianus*). This deer may have occurred in northern California prior to 1900 (records are unclear), but, if so, it has been eliminated from the state. It differs from the Mule deer in size, in antler branching, and tail configuration. Map 47.

Map 45

Map 46

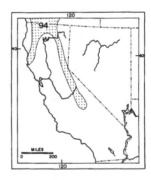

Map 47

174

Suggested Readings

A Field Guide to Animal Tracks, by O.J. Murie. 1974. Houghton Mifflin Co., second edition, pp. xxi + 375.

A Field Guide to the Mammals, by William H. Burt and R.P. Grossenheider. 1976 (third edition). Houghton Mifflin, pp. xxvii + 289.

Book of Mammals. 1981. National Geographic Society, vol. one, A-J, vol. two, K-Z.

California Mammals, by E.W. Jameson, Jr. and Hans J. Peeters. 1986. University of California Press, pp. xi + 403.

Checklist of the Vertebrates of the United States, The U. S. Territories, and Canada, by R.C. Banks, R.W. McDiamid, and A.L. Gardner. 1987. U.S. Department of Interior Fish and Wildlife Service Resource Publication 166. 79 pages.

Mammals of California, by L.G. Ingles. 1947. Stanford University Press, pp. xix + 258.

Mammals of Deep Canyon Colorado Desert, California, by R.M. Ryan. 1968. The Desert Museum, Palm Springs, California, pp. x + 137.

Mammals of Lake Tahoe, by R.T. Orr. 1949. California Academy of Sciences, pp. vi + 127.

Mammals of Nevada, by E.R. Hall. 1946. University of California Press, pp. xi + 710.

Mammals of the Pacific States, by L.G. Ingles. 1965. Stanford University Press, p. xii + 506

Mammals of the San Francisco Bay Region, by W.D. and E. Berry. 1959. University of California Press, California Natural History Guides, 2, pp. 1-72.

Mammals of Southern California, by E.S. Booth. 1968. University of California Press, California Natural History Guides, 21, pp. 1-99.

Mammals of the Southwestern United States and Northwestern Mexico, by E.L. Cockrum and Y. Petryszyn. 1993. Treasure Chest Publications, Tucson, pp. 1-192.

The Audubon Society Field Guide to North American Mammals, by J.D. Whitaker, Jr. 1980. Alfred A. Knopf, pp. 1-745.

The Mammals of North America, by E.R. Hall. 1981. John Wiley & Sons, 2 volumes, pp. 1-1181 plus others.

The Natural History of Año Nuevo, by B.J. Le Boeuf and S. Kaza, editors. Boxwood Press, pp. xi + 425.

Wild Animals of North America. 1979. National Geographic Society, pages 1-406.

Index

Names in boldface type are the major species of this book. Names in italics are those listed in the related species section. All are the "common names" that occur in the publication cited in the earlier pages. The names that are given in normal type have been used in other publications, or are in common usage that may refer to the mammal indicated.

Unfortunately, common (or vernacular) names are not always readily associated with a given species, plant, or animal. In some cases, a single species is known by as many as 30 different "common" names, often depending upon where the species occurs. Further, a single common name may be used for widely differing species, especially in different parts of the world. For example, most zoologists restrict the common name "antelope" to various Old World near-relatives of our bison and bighorn sheep. The North American "antelope" is not a near-relative and is generally referred to as a "pronghorn."

177